GAMEKEEPING AND SHOOTING
FOR AMATEURS

OTHER BOOKS AVAILABLE

Famous Foxhunters
Daphne Moore

A Hunting Pageant
Mary S. Lovell

Ferreting and Trapping for Amateur Gamekeepers
Guy N. Smith

Ratting and Rabbiting for Amateur Gamekeepers
Guy N. Smith

The Sporting Shotgun
Robin Marshall-Ball

Modern Wildfowling
Eric Begbie

Pheasants and Their Enemies
Dr. J. O'C Fitzsimons

Moles and Their Control
Guy N. Smith

The Notorious Poacher
G. Bedson

Hawks and Practical Falconry
J. E. Harting

Cockfighting and Game Fowl
H. Atkinson

Gamekeeping and Shooting for Amateurs

By

GUY N. SMITH

THIRD EDITION

Drawings by Bob Sanders

Distributor:
SAIGA PUBLISHING CO. LTD.,
1 Royal Parade, HINDHEAD, Surrey
GU26 6TD

SPECIAL NOTE

Legislation on Field Sports is under constant consideration and, therefore,
readers are advised to obtain the latest information before purchasing or
using guns and equipment.

Printed in Great Britain
by Broglia Press, Bournemouth

TRIPLEGATE LTD.,
1 Royal Parade, Hindhead, Surrey,
GU26 6TD, England

Contents

To all those who have accompanied me on
the Black Hill, in fair weather and foul

AUTHOR'S PREFACE TO SECOND EDITION

Since "Gamekeeping and Shooting for Amateurs" was first published, I have moved to live on my shoot, the Black Hill, in Shropshire. Consequently, I have achieved a personal ambition many years before I had anticipated doing so. I had often supposed, during my career in banking, that I would come here when I retired. Had this been the case, then I should not have been able to enjoy a fully active gamekeeping hobby. I remember a colleague of mine who had plans for his own retirement at the age of 60. He died suddenly at 57, and everything that he had worked for had come to nothing. Planning for the future is precarious. If you want to do anything special, then go ahead and do it. Next year might be too late!

I feel that I have been able to add much worthwhile material to this revised and enlarged edition. Whereas previously, my gamekeeping and shooting outings had been restricted to once a week, I am now out and about in field and covert daily. I have been able to experience the duties of a full-time gamekeeper, maintaining tunnel-traps and snares on a regular basis, as well as rearing game.

Consequently, we have become virtually self-sufficient as far as meat is concerned. Rabbits and pigeons are our mainstay. Prepared and cooked in a variety of ways, we avoid a boring diet. Game and wildfowl in season have replaced the conventional Sunday joint. It is well worth noting here, that wild meat has far less cholesterol than artificially reared beef, lamb or pork.

It is hoped that this edition will provide the amateur gamekeeper, rough shooter, and wildfowler with a sound basis for his chosen sport. However, no book can replace practical experience, and the more time the reader spends out on his shoot or marsh, the sooner he will become proficient at his chosen sport.

Guy N.Smith
Black Hill,
Clun.

Author in Shropshire/Welsh border hills

Introduction

During the course of my career in amateur gamekeeping, I have come to know, and made friends with, many professional keepers. They are a grand bunch of men on the whole. Once they get to know you, and see that you are a genuine game-preserver, interested in learning all you can without trying to tell them their own job, then they are the best friends that any shooting man can have.

Unfortunately, there are a number of amateur "keepers" who like to talk to keepers, and then show off their "knowledge" to others. Once the keeper learns that he is being used to boost the ego of such a man he will part with his hard-earned experience no more. It is, therefore, often necessary for a novice to "prove" himself, before gaining his chief adviser's confidence.

Most of my own knowledge came from professional gamekeepers initially. To the general public they may seem taciturn and unfriendly, but one must remember that they are a different breed of men altogether. They have no fixed hours of working, their job is never finished, and if they give the impression of being the "Ogre of the Woods" it is because the average person does not understand what harm can be done by trespassing in private woodlands. A man whose living depends on the numbers of pheasants that he can put over the guns next season is hardly likely to be polite to some erring stranger whose dog is hunting his woodlands, disturbing sitting birds.

A good gamekeeper is never popular with everybody. If I was employing a keeper and nobody had a bad word to say about him, then I should be suspicious. I would be certain that he was lacking in his duties somewhere, probably to do with the control of trespassers, and maybe even turning a blind eye to one or two of the local poaching fraternity. In general, apart from those who are directly involved in some form of shooting, everybody's hand is against the keeper. New laws are constantly being passed to limit his scope, and make life harder for him. Much harmful vermin is now on the protected list, and methods of killing these enemies, which his father before him used, are being made illegal.

Actual living conditions for the professional keeper, however, are much improved. He is no longer the estate servant that his predecessor was, fearing lest a wrong move might cost him his job. His employer is usually a much more reasonable man than he would have been pre-war, and is prepared to work in with his keeper, talking over their problems together. Wages, although still well below that of his counterpart in the industrial areas, are much improved. Usually, he has the use of a vehicle, possibly a Land Rover if he is fortunate. He is no longer the hermit of the fields nowadays, and plays a useful part in the protection of the countryside in general, apart from his contributions to the shoot which employs him. I once pointed out to a confirmed "anti" who swears by the "balance of nature" that were it not for gamekeepers then many of the non-sporting birds of our fields and woodlands would perish, perhaps some would even become extinct. How many songsters have been saved a miserable death by starvation in severe weather, or been spared from the predator which would otherwise have devoured them, had it not been for their friend the keeper?

I know of several keepers who have taken up the profession late in life. By this I mean aged about 30, having been employed in other walks of life up until this age. At one time a keeper began his career at the age of 14 when he left school, and learnt the job as an apprentice. Many of the keepers who have had a lifelong experience in their job, shake their heads in dismay when they hear that a "late-entrant" has been employed on the next estate. However, the few latecomers that I know seem to be making a pretty good job of it. One stepped straight into a single-handed post on a 2,000 acre estate over five years ago, and still has the job! Naturally, these men have done some part-time keepering before, and they go into their new career with their eyes wide open. They lack only practical experience, and employers of such must be prepared to accept a few blunders early on, within reason of course!

Every amateur keeper takes on the same responsibilities as his full-time counterpart, whether he be a tenant, keepering for himself, or a part-time vermin killer for a syndicate who do not consider it worthwhile employing a professional. If you are your own keeper, then the only advantage will be that you are your own boss. You will have to take the same kicks from the general public, and if you put a foot wrong they will be waiting to pounce on you. The only consolation is that you will not have a "roasting" from your boss for failing to hatch a clutch of pheasant eggs! The main thing is to keep within the law, and you can face anybody then. If you are on good terms with a professional gamekeeper then you have an ally worth all the books ever written on the subject, and if you succeed in making your ground into a reasonable shoot by your own efforts (and his advice!) then you will know the sweet taste of satisfaction. You will have won, and it will have been well worth it.

A modern gamekeeper's house, so different from the old-style cottages once used.

CHAPTER 1

Buying and Using Guns

CHOOSING A GUN

When you decide to purchase your first gun, you are about to make one of the most important decisions of your whole shooting career. Indeed, success or failure may depend upon the initial choice of your weapon. The man who buys the first gun he sets eyes upon, with a "that'll do" attitude, will, more than likely, be trading it in part-exchange for fishing-tackle, or a set of golf-clubs, within a year, totally disillusioned with shooting as a sport. His inability to hit anything with an unsuitable weapon he will blame on his own inaptitude, and try something else.

The most important point to observe when buying a gun, is that it "fits" you, in much the same way that you would expect a suit of clothes to fit. The stock must be of the right length so that the mounting of the weapon is a natural process. If it seems clumsy, then that gun is not for you. The only way to be certain is to allow a *reputable* gunsmith to give you a free-fitting. Once you are aware of your measurements, you can then give some thought to bores and makes.

Shotgun calibres are determined by the number of spherical balls of lead which are required to make up one pound in weight, each ball having the same diameter as the bore. For instance, an 8-bore is designated by a 2 oz. ball of lead, a 12 bore by $1\frac{1}{2}$oz, and so on.

All bores have a standard chamber length of $2\frac{1}{2}$ in., although this is modified to suit certain models. For instance, a wildfowling magnum has to take a longer cased cartridge with a heavier load. The standard shot loads for the various gauges are as follows:

12 gauge—$1\frac{1}{16}$ oz.
16 gauge—1 oz.
20 gauge—$\frac{3}{4}$ oz.
.410 gauge—$\frac{3}{8}$ oz.

5

The 12-bore is the standard game gun in this country. It is capable of dealing with all species from snipe to wild geese. However, should you favour the lighter 16 or 20 bores, then you must bear one thing in mind. The effective killing range is virtually the same, only the shot pattern is smaller, and a greater degree of marksmanship is necessary. The 16-bore is preferred on the continent, and there is very little difference between this and the twelve. I have, amongst my own collection of guns, a unique German sixteen, incorporating a $7 \cdot 3$ mm. rifle barrel beneath the other two barrels. It is in exceptionally good condition, and worth about £500. I occasionally use the shotgun, but my firearms certificate does not permit me to purchase ammunition for the rifle. I presume that the weapon is designed so that a wild boar can be dealt with effectively, if one happens to be flushed on a pheasant drive.

I have always been fond of the 20-gauge. It is light, hard hitting in the hands of a good shot, and does not weigh heavily under one's arm on a hard day's walking. Yet, I am always of the opinion that it is more for the *experienced* man, he who is getting on in years, and is grateful for its lightness, or for a lady-shot. Therefore, I say start with the conventional twelve. If you can't use that, you won't be able to use anything!

Having decided thus, the manufacturer of your gun is of no small importance. Nowadays, there are a variety of brand new foreign guns on the market at prices below that of their English counterparts. Some are good, some indifferent and others very bad. I have experienced two of the latter. The first would not pattern properly, and the ejector on the second broke the first time I used it! On the other hand, I know several people who have used a foreign gun for years, and it has proved reliable throughout.

ENGLISH GUNS

Of course, good English guns are an investment. They are recognised throughout the world as a hallmark of quality. If you've plenty of cash to spare you won't regret spending a few thousands on a Purdey "best". However, this being the exception rather than the rule, one must try to find a good sound model at around £300. At this figure you will be buying something worthwhile, a gun which will last your lifetime, and possibly that of somebody else afterwards.

"Bargains" are to be treated with suspicion, unless you know the vendor well, in a private sale. Nobody, knowingly, sells good guns cheaply today. They know, only too well, that they could

Belgian folding single-barrel .410. An ideal poacher's weapon, fitting easily beneath a coat or nestling in a ''hare'' pocket

Photo: Lance Smith

Belgian folding single-barrel .410

Photo: Lance Smith

Plate 1: A Rabbit in view

Plate 2: Pheasants in the Autumn

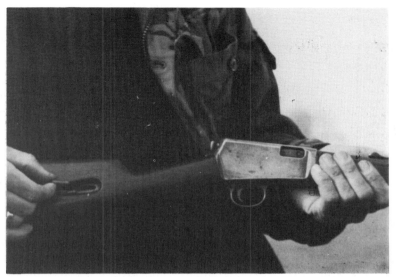

Winchester model 1903 .22 automatic rifle. Tube in stock feeds magazine. An ideal weapon for the amateur keeper Photo: Lance Smith

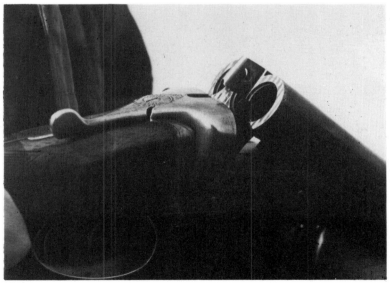

12-bore. 26 in. barrels with 3 in. chambers. Suitable for both game-shooting and wildfowling Photo: Lance Smith

16-bore. Manufactured by Thieme & Schlegelmilch, Suhl. Incorporates a 7.3 mm.
rifle. Designed for game and wild boar shooting

obtain the full value without any trouble at all. If, however, you do decide upon a private deal, then a very thorough examination of the gun is vital before you part with any money. If possible, try to take it to a gunsmith before you clinch the deal. The law today protects the buyer, but if you foolishly buy it on the spur of the moment from a casual acquaintance, and then are unable to find him again afterwards, there isn't much you can do about it. Anyone who sells a gun which is currently ''out of proof'' is liable to prosecution, whether he was aware of the fact or not. There again, your gunsmith is the best person to advise you on the validity of these markings on the barrel.

"Made to measure" Guns

Some men prefer to have their guns made especially for them. In effect, this is no dearer than buying a weapon off the racks, unless, of course, there is to be some unique feature incorporated. I had my own gun made for me by the Midland Gun Company Limited, Birmingham (taken over by Messrs. Parker Hale) in 1960. I designed this myself, some two years prior to the order being accepted, and began contacting gunmakers throughout the country with a view to obtaining the most reasonable price. My idea was unique, but was widely rejected to begin with. I required a combination of a game-gun and a wild-fowling magnum. I have always been an advocate of short barrels (26 in. as opposed to the standard 28 or 30 in.) yet I wanted to be able to fire 3-in. cartridges in it if the necessity arose. All that was required, in fact, was a strong action, which meant putting weight into what would normally have been a light gun. The balance need not be affected. The gun must be ''stocky'' rather than ''slim-line'' to illustrate my point simply. Wildfowling guns usually have barrels of 30/32 in., a belief from the days of black powder that length increases killing range. Actually, with modern smokeless powders, it is the degree of choke which governs this fact.

Those gunsmiths who, somewhat reluctantly, were willing to make my gun, quoted prices ranging between £125 and £350. I hesitated over the various quotations until the Midland Gun Company surprisingly agreed to carry out my wishes at the very reasonable cost of £80, which included a carrying case! For some reason the tubes had to be imported from the U.S.A., which meant that the completion could not be guaranteed in under six months. Nowadays, a conventional shotgun would take at least a year.

The makers were the epitomy of tact. They adhered strictly to the blueprint which I supplied, without comment, and within a week of the opening date of the shooting season, I obtained delivery of the gun which has served me faithfully ever since.

FIRST DAY WITH NEW GUN

It was fitting that, on the next day, I was departing for the Solway Firth on my annual wildfowling foray. My gun would receive its baptism in the very conditions for which it had been designed. Scepticism was rife amongst my fellow fowlers on the merse. Before I had even fired a shot I was blatantly told by an old-timer, "them barrels are too short. Them'll never reach the geese. No power."

I was not to be discouraged, even though I did not so much as touch a feather with my first four shots at high-flying mallard. Yet, my moment of triumph was to come before the end of that week. It was a mild, dull morning as I stood amidst a cluster of gorse bushes on the edge of the saltings. A few skeins of geese were coming off the mudflats, gaining height rapidly as they approached the inevitable line of guns, a gauntlet which they were accustomed to running, night and morning.

I was loaded with AAA shot, and as a small skein passed, some eighty yards to my left, I chanced a shot with my left barrel. I could hardly believe it when I saw the leading gander suddenly fold its wings, and plummet earthwards. It transpired that a single pellet had taken this Greylag goose beneath the beak, killing it stone dead!

A fluke? Perhaps, but I was to silence my critics a couple of days later when I killed another high bird, much more emphatically this time. As far as I was concerned, my theory had been proved, and during the remainder of that season I also shot game very consistently with my gun. My dual purpose shotgun was the success which I had dreamed about.

Now that you have finally decided upon, and purchased, the weapon of your choice, there are two more important factors which you must bear in mind:

1. To clean and maintain it.
2. To shoot with it to the best of your ability.

CLEANING

First, guns are worn out, not by use, but by *neglect!* Regular cleaning is a must every time you take your weapon out, in fair weather and in foul, whether you actually fire it or not. A close watch must also be kept for small dents which may appear in the barrels. An accidental knock against the car door, whilst preparing to set off for the day, may result in a slight indentation, virtually unnoticeable. It is easily removed by a gunsmith, and is best done so without delay. A burst could result months, even years, afterwards, if nothing is done about it. I always use a rod and wool mop for the inside of the barrels, but ensure that any surplus oil is removed before taking the gun out again. A thin film of oil is apt to spoil the pattern of one's shot, something which I learnt by experience in my very early days. I could never understand why I nearly always failed to score with my first shot of the day. It was a shooting-instructor who finally enlightened me upon this point. Wire mops are to be avoided whenever possible, or the interior of your barrels will soon show evidence of their use.

LEARNING TO SHOOT

We now come to the next stage of the lengthy preparation for a shooting career—*learning to shoot!* Unless you can shoot

Never shoot where you cannot see

reasonably well, you won't obtain much pleasure or satisfaction from your chosen sport. Admittedly, there is little to compare with a day spent in the countryside, a complete relaxation from the pressures of everyday life, but all this will be marred if you miss everything that comes within range of your gun.

There is no doubt about it, a reputable shooting school will provide the finest grounding in shotgun marksmanship available. A course of lessons will instil into the beginner how things *should* be done, and whether or not he adheres to the correct procedure, at least he will know right from wrong. However, if either you cannot afford to attend one of these places of instruction, or have not the time available, then there are certain things you can practise by yourself which will be a considerable aid to your performance in the field.

I learned to shoot the hard way, at the age of seven, under the supervision of my father and a farmer friend. My gun was an ancient .410 with a skeleton wire stock, which had been confiscated from a poacher, many years before. For three years, I went out with my father and this man, every Saturday afternoon, carrying the gun *empty,* the cartridges remaining behind in the house. Each time a pheasant or rabbit broke cover, I swung on to it with my little gun, squeezing the trigger at the appropriate moment. In this way I learnt the key to success in every aspect of shotgun shooting—*continuing the swing after the shot has been fired.* It is not easy, for instinct, at first, prompts one to halt the steady movement after pressure has been applied to the trigger. Consequently, one shoots *behind* the moving target every time. However, once the correct method has been instilled into the pupil, he will remember it for the rest of his life, just as one never forgets how to swim. Constant practice, though, is necessary to maintain any degree of consistency.

Once having mastered the art of swinging, the next step is to put theory into practice, and there is no better way to do this than to have a shot at some clay-pigeons. If you cannot borrow a trap locally, then it is best to purchase either a "hand-flinger" or its successor,a device which propels empty beer-canisters into the air by means of a small detonator. Whatever the target, it is all good practice. Of course, you will need a companion to assist you, taking turns to shoot and operate the target-launcher.

Many shotgun enthusiasts have a preference for clay-pigeon shooting over game-shooting. However, the average sportsman enjoys a shot at clays, from time to time during the close season, in order to keep his eye in. There is one main difference between the two sports. A clay target will maintain its line of flight, *decreasing* in speed after it has reached its apex. Of course, it should have been smashed to smithereens long before then! On the other hand, the live bird is *increasing* its speed, possibly swerving and jerking in flight at the same time. I am apt to regard the shooting of clays as invaluable practise in the art of handling a shotgun, and improving one's *swing,* rather than learning to kill a bird on the wing.

I have never had an incentive to shoot clay-pigeons regularly. I am not averse to a few practise shots at a village fête, yet to fire off a couple of boxes of cartridges every week I would find boring, and very expensive. All the same, this branch of the sport has a tremendous following, as the increasing ranks of the Clay Pigeon Shooting Association proves. It is a good thing, for the increasing population, and decreasing areas of our countryside, would not allow space for every one of these enthusiasts to carry a gun in search of live game.

So, having bought a gun, learned how to maintain it and studied the art of marksmanship, we are now ready to explore the wonderful world of Nature. A great adventure lies before anyone contemplating a shooting career, and only a full study of the birds and beasts of the wild will enable one to obtain the maximum satisfaction from their chosen sport.

CLOTHING

Having decided upon your gun and cartridges, one must give some thought to the type of clothing to be worn whilst out shooting. I do not intend to dwell here upon the specialist waterproofs necessary for wildfowling as this will be dealt with in a later chapter, but rather to outline the most suitable garments to be worn during the course of an ordinary day's shooting.

Clothing should be durable, comfortable, and blend as much as possible with one's surroundings. The most important thing to remember is that during the course of the season you will be shooting in a variety of weather conditions, and therefore a number of different garments will be necessary in order to combat heat, cold and wet.

A hat is a necessity at *all* times. In fact, it is the most important item of camouflage for it shields the whiteness of the face from oncoming birds, and helps to break up the outline of the body. A deerstalker is an ideal choice, the peaks protecting the face and the back of the neck from the rays of the sun, plus the fact that the flaps can be pulled down over the ears during a long cold wait for duck or pigeon. Any good soft hat with a fairly extensive brim should suffice, although I find the American-type caps rather extraneous to the conventional British sporting scene.

There are a number of excellent lightweight shooting jackets on the market today, designed for comfort during almost any type of shooting. However, one must ascertain before purchasing one of these that there is sufficient ventilation, particularly in the region of the armpits, for perspiration is equally as uncomfortable as

15

Safety: Man in front with barrel(s) pointing to ground. Rear man with barrel(s) pointing skywards

being soaked in a sudden shower of rain. Mostly they are described as being ''shower-proof'' which usually means that they will withstand drizzle. It is as well to carry a spare in your car for a change at lunchtime.

I would wholeheartedly reject any suggestion of wearing the PVC-type waterproofs sold in ex-government surplus stores. They certainly perform the proclaimed function, but they are far from comfortable to shoot in, and one becomes unbearably hot on the coldest of days.

Likewise, trouser material can produce the same discomfort if not chosen with care. Tweeds are ideal, and I would strongly advocate plus-fours in preference to any other style. Their natural ''bagginess'' means that they do not cling to your legs when the material becomes soaked, and if you have forgotten to bring a change of clothes with you for the drive home, then a couple of sheets of newspaper pushed inside will probably save you from a severe chill or worse. They may be out of fashion amongst the modern shooting fraternity, but, take it from me, if it's comfort you are seeking, you can't beat 'em!

FOOTWEAR

Footwear is probably the most decisive factor of all with regard to your performance in the field. Your footwork is a vital part of your marksmanship, and if you stumble about all day in a pair of uncomfortable, ill-fitting boots, you won't hit much at all. Rubber boots are most popular today, they don't take any cleaning other than an occasional bucket of water thrown over them, and they are easy to slip on and off. Nevertheless, the initial expense and irksome maintenance of a pair of *real leather* boots will pay handsome dividends. They will outlast three pairs of rubber boots, and most important of all you will have ankle-support, something which is sadly lacking in lightweight shooting boots. I twisted my ankle at a very early age whilst wearing a pair of the latter, and the weakness caused by an unnecessary fall has plagued me ever since.

Clothing and footwear are not of secondary importance to the choice of gun and cartridges. They are an equal part of the equipment necessary to the making of a good sportsman.

17

CHAPTER 2

Working Dogs

A GUNDOG IS A NECESSITY

Shooting without a dog is akin to sailing without a rudder. No man worth his salt will set forth with a gun without the companionship of a dog, whatever its species. If he does so, then a large percentage of the game in the vicinity will elude him. The pheasant, rabbit or hare, will squat whilst he walks within yards of them, totally unaware of their presence. More important though, wounded game will not be gathered. Instead, they will die a lingering death, long after the ''sportsman'' has retired to bed for the night. Far better would it be, in that case, not to shoot at all!

There are a variety of working dogs which will not only assist the true sportsman, but will become an inseparable companion. Labradors, retrievers, red-setters and pointers are to name but a few. Jack Russells, although I know of odd ones which will retrieve game, are more suited to the specialised rabbit-shooter. By nature, their jaws clamp together fiercely on any fur or feather which they retrieve, and this does not enhance the appearance of it on the table!

I have always looked upon labradors as the ideal, general purpose rough-shooter's working dog. I favour the yellow variety, but this is only personal preference. They are hardy, strong swimmers, have a good nose and, above everything else, they have a wonderful disposition.

The animal that will drop to shot is wasted. All he requires is one that will come to heel when called, flush his game and retrieve it. The dog which will hunt down a strong runner (i.e. a pheasant only very slightly wounded), is worth every penny of his keep.

I have had experience of both buying a ready-trained dog, and purchasing a pup at twelve weeks old and attempting to train it myself. Although Remus and Simon, my two ''ready mades'' are stalwart warriors who seldom fail me, I think a pup which grows

18

Labradors are strong swimmers

Photo: Guy Smith

into one's ways, rather than having been thrust into them later in life, is preferable. The old saying that "you can't teach an old dog new tricks" is so very true. The older dog will perform in the manner in which he was originally trained, no matter how much one tries to instil new ideas into him.

Labrador ready to go   Photo: Guy Smith

SELECTION AND TRAINING OF GUNDOGS

I am not referring here to dogs capable of becoming field-trial champions. My aim is simply to help the novice to choose a dog which will be suitable to his own particular type of shooting. It need not necessarily be of a pedigree strain. Occasionally, mongrels make quite good shooting dogs although the chances of success are greater if the animal shows clear signs of having originated from one of the recognised breeds. All that your dog will be required to do is to scent a bird in cover, flush it, and then retrieve it. The animal must be fairly hardy, and not afraid of water.

20

Spaniel makes an ideal gun dog

Photo: Lance Smith

We can dismiss pointers and setters for they are not really a rough-shooter's dog. Basically, the choice rests between a labrador and a spaniel.

TRAINING

It is advisable to purchase a pup at about ten weeks. Don't forget its injections or you may have cause to regret the omission within a very short time! You must be prepared to devote a good deal of your spare time to elementary training, obedience being the first and most important lesson. If training classes are held in your locality then the job will be made very much easier for you. Otherwise, it is a good idea to consult a professional gamekeeper who usually has a pretty good idea about training even if he is not a gundog enthusiast himself.

A suitable dummy with which to practise is essential. I have always made mine from rabbit skins stuffed with old rags. The scent will be familiar to the dog in later life, and if you keep to the same dummy the dog will recognise it throughout all the lessons.

Keep the lessons simple. Obedience is vital. It must learn to sit at the command, and remain thus until told to do otherwise. Lessons should be short and frequent, as lengthy ones will only induce boredom. Like children, a puppy's powers of concentration will not last for any length of time.

The first time that you take your dog out for the "real thing" will be a trying experience for both of you. You must be patient, and just because he appears to have forgotten everything which you taught him on the lawn at home does not mean that he isn't going to be any good. It is all new to him. He is in a different environment.

One of the best tests that any dog can have is to be taken pigeon-shooting, tied up in the hide for most of the day, and then allowed to retrieve a few birds towards the end of the proceedings. By doing this he has learnt that every time the gun is fired he cannot go charging off searching for something to retrieve. He must wait for the command. Also, he is becoming accustomed to having a gun fired over him at close quarters.

CANINE INTELLIGENCE

I remember one instance when my own dog, Remus, showed an amazing example of canine intelligence, and paid the penalty for it. It happened one August Bank Holiday when I was competing in some Gundog Water Tests. At one stage, Remus was leading with a maximum number of points. Then came the finals. A dummy was thrown into cover on the opposite bank of the wide river, to which dog and handler stood. At a given signal, the dog was sent to swim the river, find the dummy and swim back with it to his master. I had no fears regarding Remus in this particular exercise, for he had successfully accomplished it on many occasions. This time, though, crowds of spectators were lined on either bank.

Remus swam the river in record time, and went straight to the clump of gorse in which the dummy was hidden. Seconds later, he emerged with it, and my spirits soared. He would win this one! Then, he hesitated on the brink of the river, as though contemplating. I whistled him, perplexed at the delay. However, instead of plunging into the current, he turned about, and eased his way through the watching crowd, the dummy still clasped firmly in his mouth. I could not understand it, and then, a couple of minutes later, I caught a glimpse of him. He was crossing the river all right, but not in the manner which was expected of him. Instead, he was *using the footbridge,* about a quarter of a mile downstream! His initiative relegated him to third in the final placings!

Care of a Gundog
The care of a gundog is purely common-sense, and requires little space within these pages. A dry towel should be carried at all times when shooting away from home, for irreparable harm can be done by leaving a wet dog in a car for any length of time. Likewise, a few biscuits will help to tide him over until his feed if you are likely to return home late.

Something which appals me, more than anything else, though, is general carelessness where gundogs are concerned. Mostly they stem from complacency, the owner being more concerned with his immediate sport than with the welfare of his dog, who is responsible for providing it for him. It is, perhaps, a good idea if we take a closer look at some of the factors which might be of discomfort to our most valuable shooting companions, and attempt to make life a little easier for them.

I often wonder how much a gundog really enjoys these shooting expeditions with its master. One always imagines that a dog which has either a glimpse of gun or shooting impedimenta soars into a state of ecstasy. The scene is only too familiar to all of us, of dogs leaping about in excitement, whilst the shooting party is attending to those final details before setting out from the parked cars. Guns which have been foolishly propped up against vehicles are in danger of being sent flying, whilst a multitude of confusing orders are being shouted at the dogs by their masters, who seem on the verge of losing their cool so early in the day. Any womenfolk who happen to be present will automatically adopt an attitude of canine defence, and pandemonium will reign for some minutes. There is no doubt that the dogs in question really do enjoy these gatherings. The anticipation of a day spent in pursuit of grouse, partridge or pheasant affords them as much pleasure as the actual day's shooting, for, in this respect, their feelings must be very much akin to those of their masters. However, when the mid-day luncheon break finally arrives, particularly in the early part of the season when the weather is warm, much of this initial enthusiasm will have disappeared. They will be content to lie in any available shade, their only requirement being a long drink of cool water, and during the latter part of the day, proceedings will be conducted at a much slower pace by both shooters and dogs.

I am not implying that the gundogs in question, whether they be labradors, retrievers or spaniels, are in any way bored with a day's shooting once the first few drives have been completed, but that which they considered to be a pleasurable outing during the first few hours, has now become a day of gruelling work. However fit a dog may be, it cannot keep up a tireless pace indefinitely, and one must remember, particularly when rough-shooting or walking up, where it is required to work through dense undergrowth, that it will traverse many more miles in a day than its master, who usually remains on the rides or paths, in anticipation of a shot. I am convinced, however, that a dog will work much more thoroughly in the latter half of a day's shooting, when it has panted away that early enthusiasm. The slower pace will encourage it to work more systematically in the immediate vicinity, rather than charging ahead, intent only on flushing birds before any of the other dogs.

CANINE DISCOMFORTS IN THE FIELD

During one August I had the task of trying to reduce the number of rabbits on my hill-shoot after a series of complaints from neighbouring farmers. Due to the nature of the terrain, and the time of year, shooting was the only solution. My method was to remain on the Forestry Commission road, whilst my yellow labrador, Remus, worked the steep banks and adjoining spruce thickets. For the first hour Remus worked tirelessly and then he became more and more reluctant to leave my heels. There were still rabbits lying in the undergrowth, but his willingness to work had lessened considerably. Whilst I will under no circumstances tolerate a lazy dog, I would never dream of forcing any dog to

Plate 3: Pheasant Chicks (2 weeks old)

Plate 4: A good day wildfowling

work when his strength is being continually sapped by excessive heat, for it will only serve to destroy any enthusiasm for the sport which is born in him, and one may find oneself encumbered with an animal which is hesitant to leave the fireside for a day with the gun in later years.

Flies are the curse of all gundogs. Whatever steps one may take to ensure the comfort of one's canine companion whilst in the shooting field, there is virtually nothing that one can do to protect him from the black swarm of these insects which will not give him so much as a minute's peace on a hot summer or early autumn day. They will follow him incessantly through field and covert, settling on him at every opportunity, their main objective being to crawl on his nose and eyes, distracting him from his work, and causing no little discomfort to the poor animal.

Excessive cold can be as bad, if not worse, than heat, from a dog's point of view. It is far more harmful, in fact, and many dogs today are suffering from rheumatic complaints which could have been avoided with a bit of forethought on the part of their owners. One reads accounts of "hardy" wildfowlers who have braved the worst of the elements to obtain a shot or two at geese or duck. Little thought is given by the reader to the rigours which the dogs accompanying these men had to undergo. I am not trying to advocate the absence of a dog on the marshes in times of hard weather, but I am strongly advising that adequate steps are taken to ensure its maximum comfort under such conditions. A sheet of polythene for it to lie on, during a long wait, takes up very little room in a game bag. Likewise, that towel, with which to dry off a dog which has been subjected to a swim in freezing water, is no problem. These are only two ideas which present no trouble to the shooting man, and will certainly pay dividends in the future. A gundog's working life will be prolonged, as well as the companionship of a faithful friend.

I once lost a goose on the Solway marshes through consideration for the comfort of my dog, Remus, but I have no regrets about it. It was on an early October evening, and as I looked out of the window, prior to setting off for the evening flight, it began to pour with rain. With the absence of wind, I had no great hopes of a shot at geese, and I decided to leave Remus behind, rather than subject him to a soaking for nothing. I crouched in a shallow creek that night, on the banks of the Lochar Water, with no protection whatsoever from the rain. As time wore on, and I became thoroughly soaked, I was glad that I had not brought my dog. At last, when it was almost time to leave, for which I was truly thankful, I heard geese somewhere in front of me. Then I saw them, a small skein, just visible in the falling darkness, within range to my left. The leader folded up to my second barrel, but somehow its impetus managed to carry it to the other side of the Lochar where it hit the mud with a resounding thump, stone dead.

I attempted a crossing, for the tide had ebbed, and the channel of water was barely up to the top of my waders. However, I had hardly reached midstream before I began to flounder in treacherous mud. I decided to retrace my steps, for a goose is not worth risking one's life for. I was bitterly disappointed, nevertheless. It would have been an easy retrieve for Remus, but I felt, even then, that it would not have been worth the consequences of a long, wet wait for him.

The question of a dog's comfort during journeys to and from shoots is worthy of mention. A dog which has been in a cramped position in a vehicle for an hour or more before arrival at the destination, cannot be expected to work well, nor can one which has been shut in a vehicle on a boiling hot day, without proper ventilation. I do not agree with dogs travelling in the boots of cars. An old rug thrown over the back seat will be much more comfortable, and the upholstery will be adequately protected.

The comfort of one's gundog will play a large part in the quality of his work in the field. It's well worth it, for kindness will pay dividends in the long run. The whole of one's sport depends upon it.

CHAPTER 3

Cartridges

RELIABLE AMMUNITION ESSENTIAL

Cartridges are, without a doubt, the most important part of a shooting man's impedimenta. Indeed, his gun, be it a Purdey or of an imported foreign make, is of no consequence without *reliable* ammunition. In order to achieve the best possible performance in the field, he must use good quality cartridges, suited to his weapon, and make a brief study of the various shot sizes recommended for the quarry which he pursues. Cheap cartridges are a shooting man's worst enemy. Not only are they liable to condemn fur and feather to a lingering death, but they will ruin a good marksman's confidence.

The most reliable way for the beginner to ensure that he starts with a good brand is to consult either his local gunsmith or an experienced friend. Failing that, leading proprietary brands will suffice until he is able to make a discerning choice, for they have stood the test of time. However, shot-sizes must be taken into consideration also, and the undermentioned table will serve as an initial guide to the young man embarking upon a shooting career:

Quarry	Shot Size	Load
Pheasant/Partridge	6	$1\frac{1}{16}$ oz.
Mallard	4 or 5	$1\frac{1}{8}$ oz.
Teal	6 or 7	$1\frac{1}{16}$ oz.
Geese	BB, 1 or 3	$1\frac{1}{4}$ oz.
Hare	4	$1\frac{3}{16}$ oz.
Rabbit	5 or 6	$1\frac{1}{8}$ oz.
Pigeon	6	$1\frac{1}{16}$ oz.

No. 6 shot is nowadays accepted as a general purpose size for game shooting, and provided that one recognises 40 yards as an *effective* killing range, then this size should suffice. A little practise in judging distances, away from familiar landmarks, would certainly prove beneficial in the long run. A word about the storage of cartridges would not be amiss, for, over the years, when shooting in company, I have often witnessed a colleague struggling to remove a swollen case from his breech. Of course, modern plastic-cased cartridges will not be subject to atmospherical conditions, but even the leading manufacturers still produce paper-cased brands which will swell if kept in a damp room. On top of wardrobes (with apologies to housewives!) is often an ideal place. After all, seldom does one hang clothes in a damp room.

HOME-LOADING

At some time or another, the "do-it-yourself" shooter will incur a desire to load his own cartridges. There is double satisfaction in bringing down that high pheasant with your very own load. You feel on a par with the country's leading cartridge-manufacturers! *They* could not have done better—in this instance, anyway!

Home-loading is not to be undertaken lightly. It is more complex than ever in this modern day and age, although the tools available today ensure a better finished product. Costs can be cut by about one-third, and providing that one has the time available, then it can certainly be rewarding.

A kit capable of loading (singly) approximately 100 shells per hour is currently on sale at around £20. If one is more ambitious, the total output can be trebled by investing something like £70 in a more elaborate device. Mostly, this latter is used by syndicates or clay-pigeon clubs whose main object is to cut costs.

The average rough-shooter is apt to regard cartridge-loading as an integral part of his hobby. During the long winter evenings, when he cannot be abroad with dog and gun, then at least he can do something to further his sport at the weekend. He will obtain great satisfaction from reloading last Saturday's fired cases in preparation for next Saturday's foray.

Cartridge-loading falls into the following stages, and must be carried out in that order:

1 De-capping fired cases.
2 Re-capping.
3 Insertion of powder.
4 $\frac{1}{8}$ in. card wad.
5 $\frac{1}{4}$ in. felt or waxed wad.
6 Another $\frac{1}{8}$ in. card wad.
7 Shot.
8 $\frac{1}{16}$ in. card overshot wad or crimped closure.

9 Turning in the end of case or crimp.

10 Re-sizing case which always swells slightly with reloading. (A re-sizer is always a handy tool to possess for use on ordinary paper-cased cartridges after a wet day in field and covert.)

That is the order in which a cartridge *must* be loaded, regardless of the type of apparatus. However, before commencing, a leaflet of loading instructions must be obtained and adhered to. Gunsmiths, or Messrs. I.M.I. of Witton, Birmingham, will be only too happy to supply one upon request. Years ago this was not necessary, and almost anyone could load his own ammunition. A few grains of powder more than the required measure would result in nothing more than an increased recoil. With modern powders, burst barrels, or worse, will surely result after careless loading.

Next to an overload of powder, a badly-seated percussion cap is a very real danger to life and limb. The cap, not having been inserted to its full extent, protrudes beyond the base of the cartridge, and, as the gun is closed, it catches on the face of the breech. As a result, the ignited cartridge will backfire into the chest and face of the shooter. It is far from a pleasant thought.

However, the careful man will soon become a proficient and safe loader. There is one controversy, though, which will never be settled amicably amongst shooting men. Should cartridges have a rolled turnover and an overshot wad, or merely a crimped closure? In theory, the card wad can, on occasions, disturb the flight of the shot, thereby spoiling the pattern on impact. In the case of the crimped cartridge, where there is no wad, this cannot happen. My only comment is that I shot very consistently with rolled turnovers for 20 years. Apart from that, I am in the hands of the ballisticians.

CARTRIDGE COLLECTING

There is another aspect of cartridges, so popular amongst the shooting fraternity today that I cannot exclude it. Namely, the collecting of old cartridges. Indeed, to many, it will probably prove more interesting than ballistics and advice on home-loading.

During the past few years I have acquired a few very interesting shotgun cartridges to add to my already growing collection. After a rather depressing "lull" in this field, it seems that there are still a few items of interest to the connoisseur which have remained hidden throughout the years since the war. I was beginning to think that saturation point had been reached, and that my only hope of obtaining those brands which have so far eluded

A collection of shotgun cartridges. Many of the brands shown here are rare items,
much sought after by collectors throughout the world

Photo: Lance Smith

me was to buy them from other collectors, at prices well in excess of their value.

I wonder how long ago it was since "Nobel's Sporting Ballistite" loaded with 1½ oz. of shot in a 3-in. case was used? Certainly prior to the war, and probably shortly after World War I. This buff-coloured cartridge has little about it to enhance the look of one's showcase, but is a welcome addition to mine, for I feel that it must be comparatively rare because in those far-off days magnum cartridges were not used to the extent which they are today. Wild fowling was mostly localised, due to lack of transport, and the hardened wild fowlers would no doubt prefer to use their own loads in brass cases, which could be re-charged innumerable times.

A rather attractive cartridge is the "Sporting Life" which was manufactured by W. W. Greener Limited of London and Birmingham. These are loaded in bright green cases, adorned with a picture of a very confident, strutting cock pheasant. I suspect that my own specimens of this particular brand came to light fairly recently when that well-known firm was taken over by Webleys, for they are in as good a condition as I would expect to find a box of modern proprietary brands. Unfortunately, mine are only in 16 and 20 bore which may account for their having remained unsold in contrast to the standard 12 bores.

I am always interested to see the once famous Eley "Rocket" Cartridge still to be found in many collections. Judging by the number that I have come across, a great many must have been sold whilst they were in production. I am constantly informed that any game shot with one of these aids to marksmanship, would at once be rendered inedible, but never having tried one out in the field, I am not in a position to confirm or deny this theory. I should think, though, that a bird which was unlucky enough to be hit by the phospherous flare would be three parts roasted before it went into the oven!

Eley "Deep Shell" cartridges, in their famous dark green cases, were a much used brand in the years prior to World War II. However, they were not always a standard load by I.C.I., as a close examination of the overshot wad will show. They were sold as capped cases to private gunsmiths, and I have some in my possession bearing the name "Aldridge, Ipswich". Often capped cases were sold stating that only the cartridge case was made by Eley Kynoch, a much safer advertisement for that worthy firm. A casual user of "Deep Shell" could easily have damaged sales in general had he been unfortunate enough to purchase some poor loading by a second-rate gunsmith.

Greenwood and Batley cartridges were always firm favourites of mine in the shooting field, and I am most reluctant to part with those remaining in my collection, since they closed down this side of their business. They were a good sound cartridge, giving reliability at all times, and the "Greenbat" powder was really a substitute for Smokeless Diamond. Greenwood and Batley supplied cases, and even loaded for other firms. Elton Stores of Darlington had their cartridges loaded by this Yorkshire firm, and certainly, in the latter years of their existence, Page-Wood of Bristol, famous for their double crimp, used G & B cases.

A cartridge which has always remained something of a mystery to me is the "Challenge". It was certainly manufactured up until fifteen years ago, and yet bears no maker's name. The illustration on the orange case is of two fighting gamecocks, and it is most definitely a Greenwood and Batley case. I never came across any shops which stocked them, and my own supply came from a bulk carton of assorted brands which I was given by a retired shooting man. I have since seen other specimens in various collections, but nobody seems to be definite about their production.

I think by far the most interesting item I found amongst my recent collectors' pieces were about a dozen, very ancient, rimfire No. 3 bore cartridges. The cases were pale green, and only the headstamp "E" provided any clue regarding their manufacture.

A friend eagerly fired one in his "garden gun" as an experiment. There was a crack, hardly louder than that of a toy cap-pistol, and a puff of villainous yellow smoke. When he opened the breech he discovered that the paper case had parted company from the brass head, and a cleaning rod was necessary to remove the former from the barrel.

I was again pleased to find a couple of my old favourite, pre-war "Maximum" and "Grand Prix" amongst this oddly assorted bunch. These have certainly stood the test of time. The powders may have varied over the years, but the name has remained. I often wonder why other famous brands such as "Primax", "Bonax", and "Westminster" were not revived after the war. They were a household name in their day, but no doubt with the limited loads required by the average shooting man, some had to go, and now they are only to be found amongst collections.

And so the search goes on, for a true collector's thirst can never be quenched. Sometimes, for months, even years, it seems that every conceivable brand that was ever manufactured has either been lost forever, or re-discovered by some lucky man who promptly locks it in his showcase, where it will remain a prisoner for posterity. Then, suddenly, one comes across an unheard of item, and the fever comes to life again. However, this is collecting, in whatever form it may take, the whole world over.

I think there is one cartridge which I would travel any distance to obtain should I ever be fortunate enough to be given the opportunity. I have never seen it, and I do not know of anybody who has, but I have heard it talked about amongst the experts. It is a blue cased, 16-bore cartridge which goes under the name of "Hollandia". It is in no way connected with Messrs. Holland and Holland, as I thought at first, until that firm advised me to the contrary. Possibly it is the one cartridge which would persuade me to retire from the collecting game, and rest on my laurels. If I could obtain it tomorrow, I would be prepared to close my collection . . . or would I?

CHAPTER 4

Rough Shooting

VARIOUS TYPES OF ROUGH SHOOTING

The term "rough shooting" is used to define an acreage over which one may shoot, but it lacks the luxury of a professional gamekeeper, crop planning for game management and many other features which go to make up those shoots where pheasants are reared intensively. Basically, it is a much more casual approach to the sport, and many prefer the relaxed atmosphere of being able to potter around with a gun at times of their own choosing.

Many rough-shooters pursue their sport on the Sabbath, something which is regarded with disdain by some conventional sportsmen. For years this has been a topic of controversy, but in all fairness it must be said that many average working men are deprived of the luxury of shooting on the remaining six days of the week, and without a foray on Sundays they would not be able to shoot at all. So long as they observe the game laws, and do not kill game on this day, I can see no earthly reason why they should not enjoy sport with wildfowl, pigeons, rabbits and vermin. Hares, I hasten to add, cannot legally be taken on a Sunday.

Rough shooting today is in far greater demand than ever before. Extortionate prices are being asked, and paid, for land which is totally unsuitable for either game or shooting. A fair price for shooting rights can only be determined by the areas in which they are situated, and the potential therein. However, on today's prices, I would estimate £1 per acre as a reasonable rent. Yet, as long as there is somebody willing to pay £1.50–£2 you won't get it for £1.

UPLAND SHOOTING*

Upland shooting is a wide interpretation of a variety of types of shooting conducted on land approximately 1,000 ft (300 m) or more above sea-level. It covers forays after ptarmigan in the Highlands of

*For fuller coverage see the author's *Hill Shooting and Upland Gamekeeping* (Saiga)

Scotland, many grouse moors, both in Scotland and Wales, and also rough shooting . . . often the roughest of its kind.

It is the latter with which we are concerned. To many sportsmen the effort may not seem worthwhile in relation to the sport, but of one thing we can be certain: every item in the bag at the end of the day will have been earned in the hardest way possible. Nothing will be easy. In a way this type of sport can be likened to dry–land wildfowling. The going will be rough, the weather often unkind, shots will have to be taken on steep slopes where one's foothold is uncertain. But the satisfaction gained from success will be all that much greater.

The Terrain
In high altitudes there will be little arable land. If one is fortunate there will be a few acres of swedes or mangolds, grown for winter fodder for sheep or cattle. Much of the land will be sparse grassland that scarcely offers enough cover for a mouse, but one redeeming feature is that many hill farmers allow their hedges to grow tall and thick to shelter their livestock from tearing winds and howling blizzards. These hedgerows will often hold rabbits just like they used to in years gone by in lowland areas before progressive farming determined that such growth was uneconomical.

As for woodlands, as likely as not they will be Forestry Commission thickets, many impenetrable, a haven for foxes and other predators. With luck there may be a small pool, hardly worth a glance, it seems, for surely duck will not flight regularly at such altitudes.

All in all, it does not look very promising, but with a little patience and an awful lot of hard work it is possible to make a good rough shoot out of such a place.

BUILDING UP A HILL SHOOT
The most essential factor is vermin control. If you have foxes and crows in abundance on your land you will not have much game. With contrasting terrain, though, it presents problems. On one part of the shoot you have open grassland with no cover, and on the other you have dense woods which you can only penetrate in places.

Well, the best way to reduce foxes is to organise a few drives. In most upland regions there are 'fox clubs', farmers and locals to whom a day spent after Reynard is their favourite sport. Many of these clubs derive their income from the sale of fox pelts, and as an added incentive they are fully aware that for every fox they kill there is a chance that one of their lambs will be spared in the following spring.

They rely on organisation for success. There are those with the terriers; the beaters who are prepared to face the densest of cover, and the guns who are generally the safest you will meet anywhere. Note

UPLAND

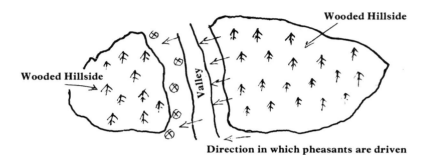

Guns stationed in the valley between the wooded hillsides. This will be a natural line of flight for the pheasants

LOWLAND

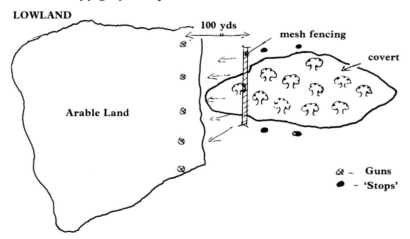

The mesh fencing will force the pheasants to take wing. 'Stops' will be necessary to prevent the birds from running out of the covert before they reach the fencing

The location of guns in high pheasant shoots

how they space themselves along forestry rides, all facing away from the oncoming beaters, at 50 yard (45.72 m) intervals. They will kill most of the foxes they shoot at, for years of such shooting has sharpened their reflexes to such an extent that a fox rarely makes it to safety across the narrowest of rides.

Contact such a club and invite them to drive your land. You will be a spectator to most of the proceedings, but with luck you might get a shot. Sometimes these clubs account for as many as seven or eight foxes on such a shoot, and they ask nothing more than to be allowed to take the carcases away to skin. It is a small price, indeed, to pay for such a good job of vermin control.

Of course, you will have to contend with members of the corvine tribe,and where the opportunity presents itself you can obtain some good shooting in conjunction with decoys and a call. An owl decoy is always a good draw for corvines, and is doubly effective if you place a crow or magpie decoy in the vicinity. Corvines love to mob an owl, and if you call right (the growling, fighting call), they will converge on you. Of course, you must be well hidden, and the edge of a Forestry Commission thicket makes an ideal hide. Wear a face mast, keep still, and make every shot count. Set up your dead crows as additional decoys, with a forked stick beneath their heads. The more decoys you have, the better the sport will be.

Another very effective method of crow control is the use of a crow trap. This is usually a 6 foot (1.83 m) square mesh cage with a tapering funnel leading down into it. This ploy works best in hard weather when food is scarce, and baited with 'lights' or butchers' scraps, it will sometimes catch up to a dozen crows a day. When there is snow on the ground, a bottle of blood, also obtained from your butcher, will prove an irresistible draw for crows. It shows up plainly and they will spot it from the surrounding hills.

PHEASANT REARING

It is a well known fact that pheasants do not like high ground. They prefer the valleys where it is warmer, and there is more food to be found. So, you must provide them with both warmth and food.

Forestry Commission woods have ample warmth, but coniferous trees offer nothing in the way of food, their thick branches killing the undergrowth beneath them. You must make these woods acceptable to game, and the only way to do this is to have well-filled hoppers that will provide a constant supply of grain.

The siting of hoppers is important. If one is placed close to a patch of undergrowth then it will not be long before the foxes realise that pheasants are using it, and Reynard will only have to lie quietly, close-by in order to secure an easy meal for himself.

Wide clearings are best for feeding points and a few bales of straw, broken up and scattered about will make the birds forage for their food. They will thus be occupied for some considerable time instead of filling their crops and then wandering off in search of pastures new.

If you rear pheasants, then release them near to one of the hill farms on your shoot. Young poults will be easy prey for vermin in the forestry, but around the farms they will often feed with free-range poultry and learn to go up to roost.

You will only kill a small percentage of the birds released, but at least you are building up an isolated stock of game in the hills. Pheasants will seldom be found in abundance in such areas, but this makes it all the more satisfying when you bag one.

DUCK SHOOTING

That pool which was mentioned earlier could turn out to be a real gem of a flight-pond, provided that duck are encouraged to visit it. This means regular feeding and sparse shooting. No pool should be shot more than once a fortnight, anyway.

I have such a pool on my own shoot, no more than 15 yards (13.72 m) long by 10 yards (9.14 m) wide, and situated in the heart of a forestry thicket. And the duck flight in regularly, in spite of the fact that there are no rivers or lakes nearby. They have simply found a regular supply of food in an isolated place where they are seldom disturbed. Food, and peace and quietness, are all that these birds ask.

One of the main drawbacks with a pool in the hills, though, is that from November onwards it is likely to become frozen for long periods. Therefore, you must make the best of September and October, and strike a happy medium between obtaining plenty of sport and over-shooting.

PIGEONS

Pigeons, often the nucleus of the hill shooter's sport when myxamatosis has depleted his rabbits, are even more of an unknown quantity than they are in lowland areas.

Often a hard spell of weather will mean that the hills are deserted of pigeons as the flocks seek the warmth and food of the lowlands, just as the pheasants do. Yet, during the spring and summer months the upland woods will be full of nesting pigeons, and some good sport can be obtained in the forests by walking the rides and flushing the birds from the thickets.

Another time when pigeon shooting can be at its best is during late July when the birds are feeding on bilberries. If you can find an open patch of heather where this fruit grows in abundance then the decoying can be of a high quality, and often superior to that on the lowland fields.

Flighting is difficult in the hills for wind direction plays an even greater part in the course which the birds take, than it does lower down. Also, the area is often so vast that even if your calculations are correct then the quarry could be 100 yards (94.4 m) either side of you.

Sometimes birds feeding on the north side of a range of hills will fly right over the range, circle, and come up to roost on the south slopes, finding the currents of air more to their advantage this way than simply dropping into the roost as they pass over it.

Lofted decoys can often prove an advantage when birds are flighting in from the fields lower down, provided that you are decoying in the roosting area. They will not change their roosts just because your decoys are in a particular area.

Winter is the most unpredictable time of all where pigeons are concerned. Often they do not use specific roosts but simply pitch into thickets which are nearest to the area on which they are feeding. Often it is useless to go to a wood just because the birds were there on the previous afternoon.

RABBITS

Rabbits, too, behave differently in upland regions. Usually they are to be found on the high slopes during summer, moving lower down with the approach of winter. Where the warrens are in dense thickets they are virtually impossible to ferret, and the only course left open to the tenant wishing to reduce his coney population is to snare them.

Forestry wire-fencing can be very convenient for it is easy to see where the rabbits are passing through, and one is spared the labour of driving in pegs for the snares. However, snares should be inspected at first light, not only for humanitarian reasons, but because the rabbit has many predators in the hills. One squealing in a snare will attract the attention of foxes and circling buzzards, both of which are abroad at the break of day in search of breakfast.

Sometimes the fox clubs will undertake rabbit drives if approached, but generally they are not so enthusiastic. You can obtain some good sport on gorse covered slopes on a sunny day if you have a dog which is not afraid of the thorns.

SAFETY

Safety is one aspect which must not be overlooked in the hills. The gun must always be on 'safe' whilst climbing rocky slopes, and if you are not familiar with the territory then it is advisable to carry a compass for hill fogs can descend with alarming suddenness. There is always the danger of getting lost and having to spend a night out in the hills, or, worse still, stumbling over a precipice. The dangers of 'fowling, except for the tides, are all there.

The hills have an appeal of their own, a remoteness that is only equalled by desolate salt marshes. It is the quality of the sport which matters, not the quantity. A cock pheasant flushed on a steep rocky slope tests your skill to its utmost, and is worth a dozen low fliers in the valleys beneath you.

The author's book *Hill Shooting and Upland Gamekeeping* covers in detail almost every aspect of this type of shooting.

FORESTRY COMMISSION SHOOTS

I would not accept any shooting without either a lease or a written agreement of some kind. I like to be able to plan a season or so ahead, when rearing game, and one cannot do this if there is doubt whether the existing verbal agreement will be renewed. I know several men who rent shooting, paying cash from one season to the next, without anything, whatsoever, in writing. There is always the chance that, having released a few batches of pheasant poults into the woods in July, the landlord may decide not to let the shooting when the season opens. If this happens, then there is nothing at all they can do about it. As for myself, I prefer to rent an acreage of Forestry Commission land on a long lease. These may not be the best shoots available, but at least you know where you stand.

From time to time one sees advertisements in various sporting periodicals inviting offers for acreages of shooting rights over Forestry Commission land. The tenders are considered on a competitive basis, and this is the only factor which might command a high rent for an otherwise very ordinary shoot. The landlords themselves are very reasonable as far as rent is concerned and, about ten years ago, I knew of 1,100 acres which cost the tenant a mere £25 per annum!

No doubt these advertisements receive a terrific response in these days when shooting is so hard to obtain. One must bear in mind, when considering forestry land, that game will be very sparse indeed. A few hundred acres of spruce and pine thickets may look very attractive, but game birds do not regard them in the same light. Admittedly, they are good roosts for pheasants, providing that the surrounding agricultural land is amenable to these wandering birds. However, the shooting-tenant of the woodlands will only stand a chance of a shot at pheasants just after first light, and with the approach of dusk, for they will spend the daylight hours in fields of rape and swede, or perhaps on an odd

A typical Forestry Commission shoot

Photo: Guy Smith

field or two of stubble in the early autumn. Partridge will favour the arable lands, anyway, and only on very rare occasions have I seen them in my own Forestry Commission woods. Grouse, of course, will at once desert those tracts of heather when tree-planting commences, and thousands of acres of grouse-moors have been destroyed in this way. My own shoot was once inhabited by both grouse and blackgame, yet, although nine acres of heather still remains in one place, the last of these species was seen there over thirty years ago, a few months prior to the start of this particular afforestation scheme.

The man who decides to rent a Commission shoot can be reasonably certain of an abundance of rabbits now that myxamatosis is not having its former devastating effect upon our coney population. Ideal protection is offered in the heart of these dense plantations for the rabbit. Although a particular area may be over-run with them, they will be difficult to keep in check, and the shooting-tenant is responsible for their control! The warrens cannot be located except by crawling for hundreds of yards on hands and knees beneath the lowest branches (possibly only a couple of feet above ground level) so gassing and ferreting is virtually out of the question. Sport can often be had, though, by working a dog through the woods whilst remaining on the rides with the gun, ready to take those rabbits which bolt across. Depending on the width of the rides, quick-shooting will be called for. It is as well to remember that rabbits mostly bolt uphill, so it will be as well to work the dog on the lower slopes whilst positioning oneself above. Snaring, too, is difficult in these woodlands, although gaps in boundary fences may sometimes be used effectively.

Hares, too, will be fairly frequently found amidst the forestry thickets, for, like the rabbit, they are very partial to the bark of young trees. Duck are often fond of a quiet woodland pool, and if one happens to be situated on your newly acquired shoot, this could be a real "gold-mine".

So now we see what we can expect on average when taking a Forestry Commission shoot. Game will be scarce, and the majority of sport will be obtained from rabbits and pigeons, a few hares and, depending on local geography, perhaps a few duck and a stray pheasant or two. Is this, then, sufficient to warrant the high rents which are forced up by keen competition? I am of the opinion that, barring extortionate rents which are the fault of the applicants who are all out to "gazzump" each other, Forestry Commission shoots are good value for money. In actual fact, one is paying purely for

Fox tracks in the snow on a Forestry Commission shoot

Photo: Guy Smith

Grey squirrels are the curse of most Forestry Commission shoots
Photo: Guy Smith

the right to carry a gun on the land, and then the rest is up to the individual. Like everything else in life, it is what you put into anything which is the deciding factor on what you get out of it.

IMPROVING YOUR SHOOT
How, then, can one improve upon an area of thickly wooded countryside, when game is a scarcity and rabbits and pigeons comprise the majority of the sport? As far as pheasant-rearing is concerned, this is only practicable when one has a certain amount of arable land on the woodland boundaries, otherwise one is merely providing a neighbour with game, and an unscrupulous man will soon capitalise on this. So, if your shoot is purely woodlands, then you will have to adjust yourself to being content with the odd wild bird, and regarding a more humble quarry, such as the rabbit, as the nucleus of your sport.

However, vermin-control, as in "game country" is just as important in these wilder places. Grey squirrels are the curse of most Forestry Commission shoots, particularly if there are a few old-established oak and beech trees amongst the thousands of firs. I have found, in many instances, that although these tree-rats prefer hardwood, they have learnt that by building their dreys in the dense thickets of these artificially planted forests, they are much safer from the attentions of the game-preserver. Consequently, the poking out of dreys is out of the question, but one very effective method is the use of humane traps situated in tunnels in the vicinity of where the dreys are thought to be. Cage-traps, too, can be successfully employed, but require more attention than many amateur game-preservers are capable of giving them.

The gun, of course, is the shooting man's main weapon in his constant war against vermin. He should never be about his preserves without it, for the chance of a shot may be offered at the most unexpected moment. Likewise, feeding, in the form of hoppers installed at certain places, is essential. If there are any wild pheasants about, then they will soon find out where there is a regular supply of grain, but, even so, tunnel-traps sited nearby will average a far greater head of grey-squirrels killed than any amount set in the woods themselves.

In my opinion, Forestry Commission shoots are ideal for the "do-it-yourself" type. There is a challenge here, and a battle to be fought and won, bringing the satisfaction that only he who has tasted success in this form will know. Wild life, in general, will benefit from one's efforts, and one will realise that everything has been so worthwhile.

CHAPTER 5

The Role of the Gamekeeper

THE GAMEKEEPER'S DUTIES

Anyone who is considering taking up a gamekeeper's job must first of all realise that this does not consist of patrolling the game-preserves all day long with gun under arm and dog at heel. There is far more to it than that.

Firstly, the beginner must be happy in solitude, often passing the day without even catching sight of a fellow human being. Secondly, there are no set working hours. At the height of the rearing season, and in those weeks prior to Christmas, there is barely even time to sleep.

A keeper's main aim is to produce the maximum amount of game for his employer. In order to do this it is vital to reduce the vermin on his beat to an absolute minimum. This must be his first task for there is no room for game and predators in any number. Years ago this would have been an all-round-the-year job combined with that of protecting wild pheasants' nests. Today, however, nearly every keeper is required to rear a number of birds by hand. Often a single-handed man is responsible for producing up to 1,000 poults, turning them into the woodlands, keeping them from straying, and then presenting them as sportingly as possible on shooting days. It is no easy job.

GROUND VERMIN

The job of the amateur gamekeeper on his own shoot is much the same as that of the professional. However, the former has the advantage of not being dismissed after a poor season. He has only himself to blame for his mistakes.

Tunnel-trapping is the most effective way of reducing ground vermin (stoats, weasels, rats, grey-squirrels) on one's land. The most important factor to bear in mind is that traps *must* be inspected *every day*. I make all my own tunnels out of three lengths of wood: (2 ft. long (60.86 cm) by 6 inches wide (15.2 cm)), forming them into two sides with a roof. Painted dark green they blend in with most backgrounds.

The standard humane traps can be set in this tunnel with ease. One does not have the trouble of removing bricks and other debris on each inspection. My last batch of tunnels lasted eight years!

Tunnels are best sited along stone walls, hedges, gateways to fields; in fact, anywhere where there is a suitable run. There is no need to bait the traps. Stoats and weasels are naturally curious creatures. They cannot resist entering any kind of tunnel when they can see daylight at the other end. A couple of sticks placed across the entrance will discourage a foraging pheasant from having a peck inside.

PROBLEMS OF WINGED VERMIN

Winged vermin present a much more complex problem. Crows can be decoyed with a rubber owl, a few crow-decoys, and a crow-call (providing it is used properly, otherwise it has just the reverse effect). The best decoys I ever had were a stuffed golden eagle and an Arctic Snow Owl. I wish I still had them!

Crows are more difficult to decoy than woodpigeons for their eyesight is much sharper, and they fly much slower, enabling them to spot the hidden shooter more easily. Therefore, greater attention must be given to the situation and construction of the hide.

Dead crows can be set up as additional decoys by the simple process of placing a forked stick to hold up the head. Do not forget, though, heads into the wind! I am always in favour of decoying on the edge of a wood, decoys placed about 20 yards (18.29 m) out on an adjoining field. Very often crows will come and settle in the trees, well within range, offering easy chances. After all, one has a job to do. . . .

Sometimes jays and magpies will show an interest in an owl decoy. However, they are often reluctant to show themselves, preferring to chatter insultingly from the dense thickets beyond.

GREY SQUIRRELS

The rapidly increasing grey squirrel is a scourge on any game preserve. It has none of the charming characteristics of the red squirrel which it has reduced almost to the point of extinction in this country. A native of America, the 'tree-rat' as it is sometimes known, escaped from captivity and bred prolifically. It has now reached the stage where it constitutes a serious menace to game, and it is the duty of everyone who shoots to reduce its numbers whenever possible. Unfortunately, the time when this creature is most detrimental to our efforts to restock with game is during the breeding season. We cannot disturb the coverts with shotguns so we must resort to a more silent weapon, and there can be no better than the .22 rifle; but in order to obtain the best results it has to be used *effectively*. It is not suficient merely to set forth with a .22 in the hope of surprising an unwary squirrel. **The reader must, of course, hold a current Firearms Certificate.**

Unfortunately, from May onwards the growth of foliage in any wood is an advantage to our quarry. A squirrel which is flushed from a drey moves quickly, and apart from the cover which is now in abundance, one is unlikely to hit it except with an extremely lucky shot. As in any other aspect of shooting, it is essential to avoid wounding and unnecessary suffering at all costs. Therefore, we must adopt other tactics.

The grey squirrel does not have the cunning of other vermin such as stoats and weasels. It is more prone to roam boldly during the hours of daylight, and once it discovers a source of easy food it will return again and again. For instance, during the long drought of 1976, the author accounted for a whole family of tree-rats over successive mornings where they were raiding an orchard.

The outside of a wood is the best place to lie in wait for squirrels, and if you are lucky enough to have a couple of woods fairly close together these creatures will cross from one to the other, time and time again. The squirrel only moves quickly when disturbed, and apart from this it will traverse the ground with many stops to explore and forage. It is then that the gamekeeper must take advantage of it.

First, it is imperative to determine not only the whereabouts, but the movements of squirrels on your shoot. Remember that, like other four-footed vermin, they are reluctant to cross open spaces except where absolutely necessary, and will take advantage of any fence, wall, or hedgerow, even if it means making a lengthy detour to reach their destination.

Reconnaissance is imperative, but it is always worthwhile taking the rifle along with you. You may be lucky and drop on a squirrels' regular run at the first attempt! These creatures usually prefer to travel along the ground, only taking to the branches when danger threatens.

Of course, dreys should have been poked out in the early spring before your birds went down to nest, but there are always a few that are either overlooked or renovated. If you are lucky enough to discover these later then you will know approximately where to lie in wait for your quarry, and having determined its possible route you must be prepared for several long vigils.

On a still day you may be able to hear squirrels moving through the undergrowth, but often their course may be determined by the chattering of jays and magpies. These corvines have no love for this creature, either, for their eggs and fledglings are not immune from his plunderings. Once you hear the screeching and chattering of these birds you must be alert, for your grey raider might show up at any second.

The moment you see your squirrel be ready to take a shot, but

mount your weapon slowly, for he has extremely sharp eyesight and is likely to spot any movement. Once he sees you, your chance of a shot will be gone.

Let us assume, then, that the rifle is mounted to your shoulder, and you have a bead on him, following his every movement. It is unlikely that he will travel for more than 10 yards (9.14 m) without pausing at least once if he has not seen you. Keep calm, and the moment he stops, aim for the head and squeeze.

It is a good idea, for practice purposes, to cut an outline of a grey squirrel out of cardboard and practice on it with your .22 rifle. Not only will you improve your marksmanship for when it really counts, but you will also learn to **judge distance.**

There is still a market for grey squirrel tails. Several firms advertise regularly for them in the sporting press. It is well worthwhile cutting the tails off any squirrels you shoot, and leaving them to dry off in an outhouse. Over a period of time, if you are proficient, you will be able to recover the cost of your ammunition. Most important of all, though, are those gamebirds' eggs and chicks which you will have saved.

TRYING YOUR HAND AT REARING

Pheasant-rearing is a complex subject. Any professional gamekeeper will tell you that even after a lifetime's experience factors beyond your control can turn success into failure overnight.

Nowadays, broody-hens are almost a rarity in many areas. This, of course, is due to modern methods of poultry farming. Thus the incubator is playing a much more vital role in the hatching of eggs. It is efficient, yet it is not a *mother* to the chicks. It relies upon man to control it. It is a robot.

If you happen to find some small-holder who still runs 'free-range' poultry then a good broody hen is half your battle. She will do the job for you with just a little kindness. After some disastrous efforts with an oil incubator, I have always searched far and wide to find a good broody. The hen must be allowed to sit on dummy eggs for a week or so before being introduced to the genuine articles. These can be substituted as you take her off the nest for her daily feed. After that, the less interference the better.

As the poults grow, one of the main curses will be feather-pecking. This is brought about by boredom, and although de-beaking is the only really effective remedy, if you can find some way of amusing them, the less your precious birds are likely to suffer from this pernicious habit. A lettuce suspended from the roof of the enclosure gives them something to peck at. Another ploy I have used is to place a couple of old mirrors inside the pen. The birds are fascinated by their own reflections, and will be kept occupied with them for hours on end.

A large enclosure for pheasants, giving the birds plenty of freedom

Pheasants showing signs of boredom, which may well result in feather-pecking. Note the provision of brushwood for nesting, in the foreground.

Special spectacles made of plastic may also be employed. Rearing under a dim light is also quite effective.

When feather pecking has started any wounds must be treated immediately. Left red and open the remaining birds resort to cannibalism on a grand scale. Painting with Stockholm tar may be effective.

A brief word about turning your birds into the woods. They are ready for release at about seven weeks. It is necessary to construct a vermin-proof (as near as possible!) release pen in the covert, so that they may become acclimatised to their future home in reasonable safety. The most essential lesson they must learn is that of going up to roost out of reach of prowling foxes. Therefore, this large wire-netting enclosure should have a few bushes or small trees within.

It is a relief to most keepers, amateur and professional, when the leaves finally fall from the trees. The months of hard work on the rearing field are now over. The results will be known after the first shoot. Or, to be more precise, hopes or fears will be confirmed. It is a hard life, but success makes it so worthwhile.

CHAPTER 6

Organising a Shoot

PLANNING IS ESSENTIAL

If it is your intention to ask a few friends to shoot with you, or perhaps you belong to a small syndicate, then some form of organisation is necessary if you are to obtain the maximum amount of pleasure from your sport. A haphazard day will surely result in a small bag at the end, birds rising out of range which would certainly have been shot with a little forethought.

Of course, it all depends on your own particular type of shoot, situation and terrain, how you go about it. Let us assume that one rents a few hundred acres of mixed arable and woodlands. One does not employ a gamekeeper, preferring to attend to the various duties oneself. In this case, the organisation of every shooting day will fall on your shoulders. Vermin control and rearing are by no means the full extent of your duties.

Beaters

Beaters present a variety of problems on almost every shoot. Gone is the day when the farm-labourer would be happy to trudge over heavy plough, and force his way through soaking shoulder-height kale for a sandwich lunch and a pound at the end of the day. You might be lucky and find the genuine enthusiast amongst your landlord's employees, but in most cases it will cost you something in the region of £5 per head for your beaters. Families and friends can sometimes be utilised, but they must be fully aware of what they are attempting to do, otherwise it is preferable to have no beaters at all, and to rely on walking-up.

First, there must be somebody in charge of the beaters, and his will be the hardest job of all. Particularly on a wet day, enthusiasm wanes, and the youths who set a good pace for the first hour will seek every opportunity to shirk as the day draws on. It is no good skirting a patch of rough cover, for that is where the birds will lie. Leggings and waterproof trousers are a must, and no undergrowth must be overlooked. Sticks must constantly tap every tree if the birds are to be kept moving forward, and a straight line must be maintained at all times. It is a good idea to have a walking gun for invariably some birds will break back over the beaters, particularly the wily old cocks in the latter part of the season who have learnt that a line of guns lies beyond the covert.

Beaters must be made to feel that they are a vital part of the proceedings rather than merely hired labourers for the day, whilst at the same time enforcing discipline. Where the bag is sizeable, it is a good idea to reward them with something to take home, even if it is only a rabbit or a couple of woodpigeons. See that they are well provided for at the lunch-break, but a too generous supply of liquid refreshment is not conducive to the afternoon's sport.

A line of beaters walking towards the guns, tapping away with their sticks, is not the simple method of providing yourself with some good shooting that you think it is. There are places where pheasants will run out of the wood before they reach the end, and it is here that you must position a "stop" to turn them back. This man need not hide himself. In fact, the more conspicuous he is, the better.

Placing the Guns
Every shoot has its best places for birds breaking from cover, but one cannot continuously place the best shots there, week after week. The fairest way is to number the stands, and for the guns to draw for places before each drive. If your syndicate shoots regularly together, then turns can be taken at the favourite stands. When guests are present they can be offered a choice of where to stand, and in the case of good shots this is immaterial. However, nothing is more galling than to have the majority of the pheasants breaking over a poor shot. This is something that must be sorted out by the host, though, and it is not my place in this book to describe devious means whereby a poor marksman can be situated away from the bulk of the hurtling pheasants.

Driving
The commonest mistake on many shoots is to attempt too many drives during the course of a day. There is an old saying that "nothing any good is done in a hurry" and never has a truer word been spoken, particularly in relation to shooting. The temptation is to cover as much ground as possible, but in so doing, with the beaters being pressed into haste, many pheasants will dodge the

line simply by lying quiet. Far better is it for a man to move steadily, looking all about him, and pausing now and then to strike a small clump of dead bracken with his stick rather than rushing past it, endeavouring to keep up with his colleagues.

Each drive requires separate preparation. Guns and beaters have to disperse to different points. A gun who has been forced to hurry will hardly have regained his breath before the first birds are hurtling towards him. However skilful he is with a gun, he will not be at his best in this instance.

So, select your drives the day beforehand. Weather conditions may force you to alter your plans at the last moment, so it is as well to consider alternatives. If you attempt to shoot every covert each week your birds will soon stray in search of quieter pastures. Many shoot owners keep a plan of their acreage, and use this to determine which woods should be shot on a particular day. Don't forget that every bird that escapes the guns is intent on finding some secluded place of refuge. If this happens to be beyond your boundary where your neighbour does not shoot so often, you could well find that half of your birds find his woods preferable to yours.

Dogs

One should never take a dog along to a shoot unless being requested to do so, and even then one must be fully confident that the animal in question will not run in to shot, or bring disgrace upon its owner in a dozen different ways. You can rest assured that the shoot to which you have been invited has managed hitherto without your dog, and it is likely to be able to do so in the future. When in doubt, leave your dog at home.

There are contrasting views in relation to picking-up. Some shoots prefer dogs to be sent to retrieve as soon as a bird is down, whilst others insist that picking-up has to wait until after the drive has finished. Both schools of thought have their drawbacks. A dog may suddenly decide that as the pheasants seem to be coming from out of the wood then it stands the best chance of catching one in there. The whole drive could be spoilt by one unruly dog. On the other hand, a wounded pheasant moves quickly, and by the time the dog is sent, the bird could be two fields away. Out of humanitarian reasons I prefer the former method. If the dog is properly trained, and has had previous experience, then its chances of deciding to enter the wood are remote. In any case, I would rather see a winged pheasant despatched as soon as possible.

WALKING-UP

Of course, not every syndicate drives its birds. The terrain may not lend itself readily to this. Personally, I prefer walking-up and I would refute any suggestion that the shooting is easier. It is all a question of what one is accustomed to. A pheasant that clatters up unexpectedly at one's feet has the advantage of surprise, and many times have I seen a bird missed with both barrels in such a situation.

Walking-up is certainly a more natural way of shooting game, and the exercise involved is refreshing to those confined in an office throughout the week. Organisation is equally as important here as it is in driving. The need for a straight line at all times is of paramount importance. Perhaps if I describe the worst day I ever experienced in this respect it will serve as a lesson to the amateur in just what *not* to do.

We were walking-up grouse on a blustery October day, and the birds were exceptionally wild as this particular moor had been shot weekly since the season opened. Our host quite obviously only tackled his shoot in one way, regardless of weather conditions, and the fact that we were walking with the wind was apparently of no consequence. Small coveys rose at a distance of a hundred yards or more ahead of us, but nobody seemed to think this unusual. However, worse was to come. This particular moor had some rather squelchy patches on it, and I was first aware of this when I found myself floundering in marshy ground. The guns on either side of me did not so much as spare me a glance, and by the time I had extricated myself from my plight, I was fifty yards behind the line. The guns were walking at such a pace that short of breaking into a run I stood no chance of catching up with them, so I resigned myself to the status of a walking-gun amongst a party of beaters, hoping in vain that a covey might break back over me. Periodically, I saw others struggling in soft ground, and within an hour of the commencement of the shoot there wasn't any line at all! Occasionally one of the dogs would put up a rabbit amongst the forerunners of the party, and for once I was glad that I was out of it! The bag at the end of the day was 2½ brace, and I consider those five birds to have been far less fortunate than they deserved! Nobody seemed to think that it had been a poor day, though.

Accidents are always more likely when walking-up as opposed to driving. Particularly in cover one has to exercise the greatest vigilance. On Forestry Commission shoots it is often only possible to walk the rides, and in places guns find themselves walking on the heels of their colleagues. Never has the need for organisation been greater than in a situation like this. On no account must a shot be taken over a colleague's head.

AT THE END OF THE DAY

A day's shooting comes to an end all too quickly, particularly during November and December when it is dark before five o'clock. If there is a suitable flight-pond on the shoot then a shot at duck is a fitting end to the day. Indeed, it may be necessary to finish up in this way if the day's sport has been poor, and in the event of a successful flight the guns will go away with a feeling of satisfaction. In my own case I regard my flight-pond as a last desperate throw to turn a poor day into a good one.

However, when darkness has finally closed in, and the weary party has trooped back to the parked cars, the host has one more responsibility. He must distribute the game, and see that nobody goes home empty-handed even if he has to do so himself. On larger shoots the task is relatively simple, and is left to the keeper. A brace of pheasants for guns and guests, and the remainder is transported to the nearest dealer.

On smaller shoots, though, it is not so easy. Imagine yourself in the position of the small host who has invited three guns, and the final tally adds up to one pheasant, one partridge, and one mallard. It has been the poorest day on record, and apart from a feeling of embarrassment at the lack of sport, one is faced with distributing the bag. If it so happens that each has had a hand in shooting one bird, then give them the species which they shot. Otherwise, you will have to rack your brains and remember who had what last time you invited them. The whole business sounds petty, but when you only rent a small shoot with very little game on it, then it can arise.

My greatest pleasure lies in giving friends an enjoyable day, and I always try to organise it according to the physical fitness of my guests. When I invite someone of the older generation I try to make it as easy for him as possible. Perhaps he can be persuaded that by standing in a certain place whilst the rest of us drive towards him is to our mutual advantage. The last thing he wants is to feel that he is an encumbrance to the rest of the party. Such minor points can add an awful lot to the overall pleasure.

CHAPTER 7

Rabbits and Hares

Most shoots in this country will have a few rabbits and hares on them from time to time. The strange factor to bear in mind, though, is that the two species will not mix in any great numbers. Country lore has it that the buck rabbit seeks out and kills the young leverets during the breeding season, and, as a result, the hares prefer somewhere to breed away from the rabbits. There may be some truth in this, but mostly I believe it is a question of grazing grounds, both disliking an intrusion on their own territory.

THE IMPORTANCE OF CONTROL

Rabbits can be an asset and a curse at the same time. They provide worthwhile sport, whether by ferreting or shooting, and will often sell for £1.50 a pair. Many shooting tenants see a means to cover their expenses, in both rent and running costs, by means of a few concerted forays after coneys. Yet, rabbits can also cost you a lot of money if you allow their numbers to get out of hand. Legally, a shooting-tenant is responsible for the damage doen to growing crops by rabbits and game, either on his own land, or by the various species *coming from it!* It isn't very hard for a neighbouring farmer to prove to officials that the offenders are coming from your woods, particularly if he hasn't got any cover of his own. Therefore, you will be well advised to keep your rabbits down, whatever the time of year.

Rabbits provide some very sporting shooting. However, in the years immediately following the initial outbreak of myxamatosis, approximately 1953–60, they were virtually extinct in many areas throughout the British Isles. Indeed, it was feared that they would become so at one time. Only too well do I remember witnessing the poor creatures in the last stages of a lingering death, and I have despatched as many as eight or nine in an afternoon whilst having a walk round my shoot.

A rabbit with myxamatosis   Photo: Lance Smith

The rabbit wasn't beaten, though. Gradually, this terrible disease became less lethal in its attacks, until a few of them actually began recovering from it. Immunity to myxamatosis followed, and a new breed of rabbits sprang up. They were less inclined to live entirely below ground as had their predecessors, and spent much of the day lying in thick cover. Perhaps instinct somehow warned them that they were less likely to spread and contract the disease in the open air, as they were in the warrens. It is fleas which carry myxamatosis, and without the opportunity to move from one rabbit to another in the close confinement of a burrow, the spread was halted. By 1965 the rabbit was on the increase again, and was becoming a matter for grave concern amongst the farming fraternity. Soon it became illegal to have an excess of rabbits on your land. A report of such an instance meant a heavy fine for the landowner, passed on to the shooting-tenant who was responsible for their control. Ministry operators were called in to such places to gas the warrens. Then, another snag arose. The majority of the coneys were living above ground in dense undergrowth, and Cymag (rabbit-gas) was not having the success which it had enjoyed prior to myxamatosis.

58

It is very nice to have a few rabbits on your shoot, but you must keep a very close watch on them. There are several methods which you can employ in an attempt to keep their numbers down to a manageable proportion.

RABBIT CONTROL WITH A .22 RIFLE

The .22 rifle has a distinct advantage over the shotgun. It is virtually silent. Those spring and summer evenings of long ago have returned, rabbits hopping about on the fields bordering woodlands, grazing peacefully; the moment that the crash of a shotgun disturbs the peace there is an instant retreat towards the warrens, and within seconds those fields are empty. The shotgunner now has a long wait in front of him, maybe half-an-hour before the first rabbit ventures forth to ascertain if all is clear.

In this way the man with the shotgun will have sparse reward for his patience. But for the marksman with a rifle it is a different story.

A sunny evening in spring or summer is ideal, and a reconnaissance of the ground beforehand is advisable in order to enable one to pick one's place of ambush, and to be in position before the rabbits come out to feed. This will save disturbing them, and having a long wait whilst they summon up courage to emerge again.

Look for not only droppings but places where the grass or growing crops have been grazed off, and take up a position within easy range of this. The rabbit is not as keen-eyed as the wily corvines, but his hearing is just as acute. One must keep perfectly still, and any fidgeting will ensure that one's quarry feeds well out of range.

Smoking is detrimental to sport, too. There is an old belief, dating back to the days of the fenmen and their duck decoys, that burning tobacco destroys one's scent. These duck-hunters were in the habit of carrying smouldering peat for this purpose. Possibly it does mask the human scent, but the noise made on a still evening in the lighting of pipe or cigarette (not to mention the fire risk!) will most certainly be a factor against a good bag.

So, having taken up a position early, one should be able to shoot the first rabbits as they emerge for their evening's feed. The report of the rifle will be negligible, and if one has also paid attention to wind direction, it is sometimes possible to kill two or three rabbits without disturbing others grazing nearby, particularly if a sound-moderator is fitted to the weapon. This accessory is a separate requirement on a Firearms Certificate.

Always retrieve shot rabbits at the earliest opportunity. They are not always as dead as they might seem from a distance, and frequently wounded conies will wriggle to the safety of the nearest undergrowth through the long grass. Also, the sight of their colleagues lying dead in the field will not encourage other rabbits to feed in the immediate vicinity.

A spinney is often an ideal place from which to shoot rabbits in preference to a larger wood, for one can usually guarantee them feeding much closer to where one is waiting. Hedgerows are also good places, but concealment is that much more difficult. One must first search for burrows in the stools and signs of feeding, and then pick a spot as close as possible to this. In these days when hedges are either uprooted, or cut back so that they do not shade the growing crops, this is often a problem, and one has to crouch in an uncomfortable stance.

Rabbits shot with a rifle are more likely to fetch a better price than those killed with a shotgun. In the case of a head shot they are commercially equal to snared rabbits.

Spring and summer are not the only times when one can shoot rabbits in this way, but during the winter one is less likely to find them feeding in abundance so conveniently. They are more prone to feeding during the nocturnal hours, lying in either burrows or undergrowth by day, and those flushed from cover are not the quarry of the small-bore shooter.

We are doing a useful job in the interests of agriculture and forestry by controlling rabbits in this way, and those of us who help out could well earn ourselves the added bonus of some invitations to shoot game during the season.

FERRETS

If you are constantly troubled by rabbits, then it will be to your advantage to keep a couple of ferrets. If looked after properly they are not the ferocious creatures commonly supposed, and are a fitting complement to gun and dog.

Management

The ferret is, in fact, nothing less than an albino domesticated variety of the polecat. Ferocious in its wild state, it becomes gentle and affectionate when handled regularly, and its temperament is determined by its management.

The hutch must be kept scrupulously clean at all times, with ample light and air, and situated in a dry place away from the direct rays of the sun. It should measure no less than 3 ft. long, 2 ft. high and 1½ ft. wide if the occupants are to be able to move about freely, and avoid being cramped. The floor should comprise of a sliding tray, filled with sand, and if this is changed regularly, at least twice a week, the problem of cleanliness will be solved. It is the hutches with plain wooden floors, which become saturated with urine, that cause the ferrets themselves to smell. Hay is ideal for bedding, and should be changed at least once a week. Hay is less likely to become saturated than straw, smells sweeter, and is warmer and more comfortable.

Alternative quarters should always be available. A sick ferret must be kept apart from its mate, and jills on heat must be confined to isolation.

Feeding is important to the health and well-being of these creatures, and simply to throw table scraps into the hutch is not sufficient. The ferret is a flesh-eater, and as such should be kept to its natural diet. Butchers' scraps, poultry heads and necks, and rabbits with the fur left on are ideal. It will appreciate bread and milk occasionally, but this must be regarded more as a treat than anything else. Clean water, of course, is essential, as it is with all animals.

The main meal should be reserved for the evening, and there is no need to alter the feeding routine when ferrets are being worked. The idea of starving the animal in preparation for a day's rabbiting will only increase the chances of you having to dig out a ferret which has lain up with its kill. If it is accustomed to being fed at the end of the day it will not become aware of its hunger until towards the close of your foray.

Training
Like gundogs, ferrets require patience and perseverance if they are to become fully competent at their work. It is best to take the old jill along on all training sessions because they will quickly learn from her. You can only supervise.

It is best to keep the jill on a line, and let the youngsters work alongside her. Where possible, give them their early training in ground that is sandy and free from tree roots, because it is inevitable that you will have to dig them out at some stage. In fact, a ferret benefits from being dug out, and will prefer to emerge on its own in future. Likewise with young ferrets it is preferable to net the rabbits rather than to shoot them on the first few outings otherwise they may become gun-shy.

Working Ferrets
There are three ways to work a ferret:

    1. Muzzled

2. On a line
3. Without either muzzle or line

Where possible the latter is best, but you must be fully confident of your ferret before trusting it to wander freely in large warrens. In order to ferret effectively, a calm day must be chosen for an assault on the warrens. Only then can one hear what is going on below ground, but don't forget that the rabbits can hear you, too, so the more stealthily you move the better. It is a good idea to visit the scene of your proposed operations on the previous day, determine where all the holes lie, and cut away any undergrowth which might hinder you if you are shooting. Purse-nets are advisable for covering as many holes as possible which are screened from your view. Netting is a surer way to make a large bag of rabbits, if that is your intention, rather than simply sport. Inevitably you will miss the odd hole beneath a clump of briars, and it is a good idea to take a colleague along to shoot those that miss your nets. Once you have a rabbit in a net you must pounce quickly, and it is difficult to try to shoot and net at the same time.

Every warrener has, at some time or other, had a ferret lie up in a large warren where it is impossible to dig. Sometimes rabbit entrails left in an open sack, and sited by one of the windward entrances to the burrow, will result in the ferret being lured from below ground. On many occasions warreners have returned at first light the next morning to find their missing ferret curled up, fast asleep, in the sack. Sometimes a ferret can be smoked out with sulphur cartridges, but perhaps the following case history will deter the beginner from trying it. I once moved a ferret which had lain up in a warren by discharging a black powder cartridge into one of the holes (having first removed the shot charge, of course!), and then blocking up every exit except one. He showed up in about five minutes, almost stifled by the poisonous fumes. However, he absolutely refused to enter a warren again from that day onwards, so I was really the loser in the end.

I have mentioned before that ferrets should be handled regularly, but it is surprising the number of people who do not know how to pick up a ferret. Always approach the creature with fingers extended towards the tail, moving slowly, almost as though you are about to stroke him. Do not show any signs of nervousness, grasp him lightly behind the head, and he will not give you any trouble. A ferret which has been below ground for some time must be approached in this way, otherwise he will either dart back down the burrow or else sink his teeth into your hand.

Purse nets in position

Diseases

The main diseases from which your ferrets are likely to suffer are distemper, ear-canker and mange.

Distemper is almost always fatal, and has the same symptoms as in dogs, discharge from eyes, shivering and coughing. *Ear-canker* is an inflammation in the lining of the ear cavity, and a discharge of wax. Scratching and drowsiness follow, and if unchecked meningitis can follow. *Mange* can be caught from and given to dogs. It begins beneath the feet, and spreads to the head.

If your ferrets should be unfortunate enough to catch any of these three diseases, *consult a vet at once*. In any case, segregate the infected animal(s).

SNARING

This is not easy for the rough-shooter, particularly if he lives any distance from his shoot. Snares must be inspected at first light, not only on humanitarian grounds, but also because if you delay, Reynard will beat you to it. He usually leaves the head as evidence of his visit!

63

He who shoots a hare shall carry it!   Photo: Lance Smith

However, if you are able to set the snares, say on a Saturday afternoon, and then return at daybreak on Sunday morning, there should be no problem. Snares must be pegged down firmly with a long stake driven hard into the ground. The strength of a desperate rabbit is quite unbelievable.

Where possible, I prefer to tie my snares to the gaps in fences and hedges where rabbits pass through. I have found this much easier, and far more effective than trying to determine which runs are well-used in an open field.

Snared rabbits usually fetch higher prices than those which have been shot. Your problems could be solved in one weekend with a hundred or so strategically placed snares. A snowy day will be of great assistance when setting your wires, as you will then be certain that rabbits are passing through the various places.

SHOOTING

There are many factors which can determine success or failure when carrying out an assault on your rabbit population in this way. If the day turns out wet, you may as well stay at home, for very few rabbits will be abroad in such weather. Instead, they will seek refuge below ground and in impenetrable cover, and even the dogs will not find many. A dry, frosty day is best. The type of terrain will determine how you tackle the job. On open grassland, a line of walking guns, with dogs working in close proximity, is the best method, for rabbits lie close. Where woodlands are concerned, the party can take it in turns to walk and stand alternately, in an attempt to drive the rabbits to a line of waiting guns. For obvious reasons, though, great care must be taken not to shoot wildly into dense cover.

The best rabbit foray which I have ever experienced lasted less than an hour. I had accompanied a friend to his shoot in a remote valley on the west coast of Scotland. He decided to try and ferret, using purse nets, as there had been complaints from the resident shepherd. I was invited to take my dog, and try for a few grouse whilst he enjoyed himself thus. However, I decided to watch him at work for a bit, but it was soon apparent that the warrens were deserted. He had brought his gun with him, and he thought that it might be more interesting to accompany me. The fact that he had only brought a mere half-dozen cartridges was considered unimportant at the time. I had some thirty-five rounds with me, anyway.

Less than ten minutes after we had started the ascent of one side

GAMEKEEPING AND SHOOTING FOR AMATEURS

of the valley, my dog was bolting rabbits from behind almost every tussock of grass! My companion had soon fired his meagre supply of shells, and so I gave him half of my remaining stock. Half an hour later, we had exhausted those, and a count revealed our bag of rabbits to be 31. Even as we descended to the parked car, laden down, scores of rabbits were bolting from the path which we had already trodden! I often wonder how many we should have killed had we had enough cartridges to have carried on shooting all day.

Two years later, I returned to that valley at the invitation of my friend. He was unable to accompany me, so, loading the boot of my car with some 300 rounds of ammunition, I set off, fully confident that this was to be my "Big Day". I walked those hills for seven hours, Remus working tirelessly throughout. I saw five rabbits in all, and killed one with my only shot of the day. That very unlucky coney, it transpired, had myxamatosis. Disease had ravaged where the gun had failed.

HARES

Hares are very different from rabbits, in many ways. Legally, they are game, and he who takes them in any way must first purchase a Game Licence, costing £6. Furthermore, they may not be killed on the Sabbath, or on Christmas Day. Rabbits though, may be taken by anyone (provided that he has the land-owner's permission), and at any time. Although hares do not enjoy a close season as such, they may not be offered for sale between 31st March and 31st July. This was, no doubt, intended to remove any incentive to kill them for gain whilst they were breeding, but is somewhat out-dated in these days of modern refrigeration and cold storage.

I, personally, do not enjoy shooting hares. Although they are capable of attaining a fast speed with the aid of their long back legs, they present a fairly easy target for a shotgun. Furthermore, they are capable of carrying shot if not hit in a vital part, and all too many die a lingering death after a hare-drive. I think, however, the factor which has largely dissuaded me from accepting regular invitations to hare-shoots, is the almost child-like scream of this species when wounded. When this happens, I am the first to dash forward and despatch the poor creature, whether or not it has actually fallen to my own gun.

However, I do kill hares on my own shoot during the course of my weekly rambles. Sport is not my objective in this case, though. First, these creatures do immense damage to the conifer thickets on my land, so I feel obliged to act in the interests of my landlord.

Secondly, I am very partial to hare on the table, jugged or roast, so I feel quite justified in shooting one or two for this reason alone.

On some of the large estates, hares are very prolific, and an average drive, after the close of the game-season, sometimes produces 300–400 head shot. Although I have stated that hares do not present a difficult target, they are deceptive, and this is often the reason that they are missed. One is apt to shoot *over* an oncoming hare. The only sure way to kill them is to aim well in front of the forelegs, continuing to bring the barrels of your gun downwards as the trigger is pressed. Often a hare shot in this manner, and missed, if it has not spotted the waiting gun before, will pull up abruptly at the sudden report. It would, indeed, be a heartless man who slew it thus with his second barrel.

Mostly, I shoot what may be termed as "mountain hares" on my upland shoot, 1,400 ft. above sea-level. There is no doubt that these are a larger, sturdier animal than their lowland cousins. They graze the sheep fields by day, sometimes feeding in the adjoining rape and swedes, and then seeking shelter in the woods by night.

The hare is an expert at camouflage. It can become invisible on a

The hare is an expert at camouflage.   Photo: Lance Smith

variety of terrain. I remember one warm September afternoon pausing to rest, and smoke a pipe of tobacco, on a grassy bank, bordering some Forestry Commission woodlands. I had not got a dog with me, nor my gun, and I must have remained there for twenty minutes or more. When, finally, I stood up to leave, a hare jumped up, less than five yards from where I had been sitting. It had been there the whole time, and I had been totally unaware of its presence, even though there was no undergrowth to hide it from my vision.

The shooting man has to try to strike a happy medium where rabbits and hares are concerned. As valuable as their presence may be, they could, within a matter of weeks, become detrimental to agriculture and forestry. He has no alternative other than to shoot them liberally. Reluctant as he may be to do this during the summer months, this is preferable to either a heavy fine, or an outbreak of disease, caused by inter-breeding. We have upset the balance of Nature over the years, and it is our duty to help rectify it at every opportunity.

CHAPTER 8

Pigeons

The woodpigeon is possibly the most under-rated sporting bird of all. It is gentle, yet, as far as agriculture is concerned, a most rapacious destroyer of growing crops, surpassing even the rabbit in its depredations. As far as the shooting man is concerned, it is only during this last fifteen years or so that the humble woodie has stolen the limelight. It is no longer regarded as just a bird at which to enjoy a casual shot in some wood towards dusk. Nowadays, there is a very scientific approach towards pigeon-shooting. The man who wishes to pursue this quarry with expertise, must study such matters as decoying, building of hides, wind-direction and feeding grounds.

THE WOODPIGEON'S YEAR
We are all familiar with the peaceful cooing of the wood pigeon. It has a soothing effect upon all who listen to it, and is in keeping with the tranquility of the countryside. It is a bird which we take for granted, yet today, in various parts of the country, it is not as numerous as we are inclined to think.

Over the years our resident woodpigeon population has been swelled during the winter months by migrant birds from the continent. During spells of hard weather immense damage has been done to fields of greenstuffs by the ravenous flocks. All out efforts, including a brief experiment with narcotics, failed to check the marauders. However, during the last few winters the 'woodie' has been conspicuous by its scarcity. Only in certain areas has pigeon control been necessary. A succession of mild winters has been responsible for this. Only in the severest weather, when sprouts or broccoli peeping through the snow are the only available food, will the woodpigeon resort to ravaging crops on this scale. It shows a preference for clover, and when this is obtainable it will feed almost unnoticed.

Mild winters on the continent mean that the flocks in those countries have no need to migrate. So, it seems, everybody is happy. The 'woodie' is content because he has ample food, and the farmer is relieved that his crops are left unmolested.

The pigeon is more active in the Eastern counties during the spring and summer months when acres of peas and beans offer an abundant food supply. Market gardening is attractive to them; then comes the grain harvest in Norfolk in August. They move on to glean the stubble before the fallen grain is ploughed in. There is more woodland, too, offering acorns and beechmast and warm roosting for the winter. This is but one example of what is happening throughout the country.

Let us take a look at the bird in question. The woodpigeon is shy and gentle. Its voracious appetite is its only shortcoming. Once the winter is over its thoughts turn to nesting at the first hint of warm weather. Thousands are caught out when winter returns with a vengeance, but they persevere. The nest is a flimsy affair, and often a thick bush is chosen in preference to a nearby tree. Two eggs are laid, white in colour, and a walk through one's nearest woodland, any time between April and August, will reveal the odd empty shell lying on the ground. Usually, this is the work of the predatory corvine tribe. The author has found eggs in a nest as late as November. The woodpigeon does not believe in wasting breeding time!

The fledglings are ugly, and it is often difficult to believe that they will grow into the handsome grey bird which we know so well. At this stage they are vulnerable to winged predators, especially the sparrow–hawk, also increasing in numbers lately, and a cluster of scattered feathers beneath the trees usually means that this bird has struck.

The crop of the woodpigeon has an amazing capacity, and often as much as two handfuls of grain or greenstuff is removed from a dead bird. Its method of feeding is to eat greedily for several hours, until the crop is full to bursting point, when it retires to rest and digest. Feeding begins at daylight, followed by a short 'day roost' in a convenient wood four or five hours later. This is followed by another spell of intense feeding prior to roosting shortly before dusk.

One item on the pigeon's menu that is not generally known is the bilberry. These berries are consumed long before they ripen, but are detected by a discoloration of the droppings. Blackberries, to a lesser extent, are eaten, but usually only when they are fully ripe and juicy. These figure in the early autumn diet, but not at the expense of more satisfying foodstuffs.

There is something traditionally British about the cooing of the woodpigeon, and the loud flap of its wings as it breaks cover. It is a bird which will hold its own for a long time to come in this ever–changing countryside of ours.

DECOYING

Decoys are an expensive item. However, one can make one's own, yet near-perfection is necessary, otherwise the decoyer would be better off with none at all, for they will only serve to frighten the birds off. There are various materials from which they can be made, but one of the most adaptable is a length of plastic guttering, for it falls naturally into the rough outline of the pigeon, requiring little bending. A dead woodie is a good guide to work from. First, cut the material roughly to the shape and size of the actual bird. Outline is not nearly so important as *colouring*. Then, using a *matt* finish (not gloss, for it will reflect the sunlight) paint your decoy as near to the real thing as possible. A wooden stick, about eight inches long, secured to the underside of your finished product, will enable you to fix it firmly in the ground. If you really want to excel yourself, a small spring, inserted between rod and decoy, will cause it to move in a very lifelike fashion in the wind.

Decoying on winter wheat. Shooter has a natural hide in ditch beneath a large tree   Photo: Lance Smith

71

A suitable hide is equally as important in the making of a good bag. Portable structures are advertised in most shooting journals, but these are costly, and unless you are shooting on several days a week, hardly worthwhile. A strong machet, and a ball of twine are really all you need. Having determined the sight for your hide, cut four stakes, and run your twine around them. Then cut some branches and various undergrowth, and tie it around your hide.

Some points to bear in mind are that your hide must blend with the background, and above all, appear *natural*. It must be roomy enough to shoot from with comfort. Often, a hide is unnecessary where there is abundant cover nearby.

The scene is set. Your hide is built, and your decoys are placed strategically about 25 yards in front of it, *heads into the wind*. You know that the pigeons have been feeding heavily on this patch of clover for the last three days, and you can expect the first ones to show up shortly after daylight. You have ample cartridges, sandwiches and flask, and, if all goes well, you will be shooting until late afternoon. During a lull, go out and pick up any birds which are lying on their backs, and clear up as many loose feathers as possible. It is a good idea to set up your shot birds as additional decoys by fixing a forked stick beneath their beaks.

Pigeons are unpredictable. If you know they are feeding in a certain area, then take immediate action. They are quite likely to have gone elsewhere on the following day.

It has been suggested that the woodpigeon population is on the decline in recent years. Greedy shooters in search of additional income have been blamed for this, but I would be inclined to regard the recent succession of mild winters as having a bearing on this situation. During intense spells of hard weather on the continent, large flocks of woodpigeons migrate to Britain. Mostly, they are hardly worth shooting except in protection of crops, for lack of food has rendered them little more than feathered skeletons. They are easy targets for the ruthless gunner, often being mown down as they cling desperately to the last stalks of a field of decimated greenstuff.

I have, on several occasions, shot pigeons in woodlands which serve purely as day-roosts for the birds. The best results here are obtained by having decoys lofted into the topmost branches so that they can easily be seen by flighting woodies. It is very difficult indeed, to place these so that they work efficiently. If you are a natural tree-climber, as my shooting colleague is, then the siting of decoys is much easier. He will think nothing of scaling a 40 ft. tree, and fixing his decoys superbly, heads to the wind. The average shooter, though, will use a set of lofting poles. These are cumbersome, and can be most frustrating. Just when you believe that you have at last got that stubborn decoy into position, a sudden gust of wind will turn it round so that it is facing in the opposite direction! I well remember my first attempt to loft decoys, many years ago. I hit upon the idea of employing a set of chimney-sweeping rods as a substitute for poles. Full of optimism, I struggled over a mile with them to my chosen wood, where I began screwing them together. Then, as I sought to push them up through the overhanging branches, they bent right over, and rested on the ground on the opposite side, resembling an inverted, and very pliable "U"!

ROOST SHOOTING

Let us now take a look at a less specialised form of pigeon-shooting, namely that of waiting at dusk for the birds to flight into woodlands.

Some years ago organised woodpigeon shooting, during the months of February and March, was a traditional Saturday afternoon fixture amongst shooting men in many parts of this country. It was an event to look forward to throughout the week, a chance to enjoy some shooting, even though the game season had closed, and for many who were not fortunate enough to have any land of their own on which to carry a gun, then it was an ideal opportunity to have a shot on somebody else's, with full permission.

Gradually, this form of sport seems to have taken a back seat in the modern shooting world, and, on looking at it from a logical point of view, it is not difficult see the reason why.

I well remember the hey-day of this form of woodpigeon control. I had just acquired my first 12-bore, a single barrel hammer-gun, and Saturday afternoons could not come soon enough for me. It was the one time of the year when my father allowed me to go on our small shoot unaccompanied, for the simple reason that he wanted the migrant flocks of pigeons kept on the move without having to take the risk of allowing some stranger the freedom of our woods. He was not particularly interested in turning out himself, so I went as his representative.

I can recall many Saturday afternoons, during the early part of the year, when I stood for hours in our draughty woodlands in pouring rain, driving snow, thick fog and anything else which the elements cared to produce to add to my discomfort. Rarely did I average more than five or six birds weekly during this time, and I went to endless trouble in lofting decoys into trees, and building hides in suitable places.

What, then, was the reason for the lack of success in general, in what, on paper, seemed to be an excellent method of keeping the pigeon population within bounds?

First, lack of organisation was largely to blame for failures, year in, year out. There was no trouble in mustering an army of guns to man these woodlands, due mainly to the fact that, even so comparatively recently as ten or fifteen years ago, shooting was as hard to obtain in my own area as it is now. The private landowners were still in residence on some estates which had not yet been split up, and they were more reluctant to allow guns in their woods to partake in organised shoots than the shooting tenants of today, who followed in their wake.

Many landowners, who were only interested in game-shooting, were quite content to leave their woods in peace and quiet whilst neighbouring spinneys and thickets were undergoing a barrage. Naturally, the birds sought out these sanctuaries where they could rest in peace, and after the initial burst of firing, the shooters who had taken the time and trouble to turn out, were denied further sport.

I am of the opinion that these Saturday afternoon shoots became nothing but a bore as the years wore on. Admittedly, anyone genuinely interested in the countryside should never reach this state of absolute boredom, but many novices must have been sadly disillusioned when they had been soaked to the skin, and frozen a few times, for the sake of the occasional shot, and possibly none at all.

There are certain woods, also, which are favoured by pigeons, and others which hold not the slightest attraction for them. I fully believe that, however much firing is going on throughout the surrounding countryside, they would be loath to use this latter cover, even if there were no guns in it at all. The all important question is where do these pigeons go when a full complement of guns is after their blood?

I believe that I discovered at least one of the answers to this mystery towards the end of my organised pigeon-shooting days. I was stationed in a wood, the acreage of which was a little under 200. There was no shortage of guns, but only part of the area could effectively be covered on account of the fact that almost half of it consisted of thick, impenetrable thickets of spruce and pine. Brashing and thinning of these trees was long overdue, and it was only possible to enter these plantations on one's hands and knees,

A good pigeon wood in snow   Photo: Guy Smith

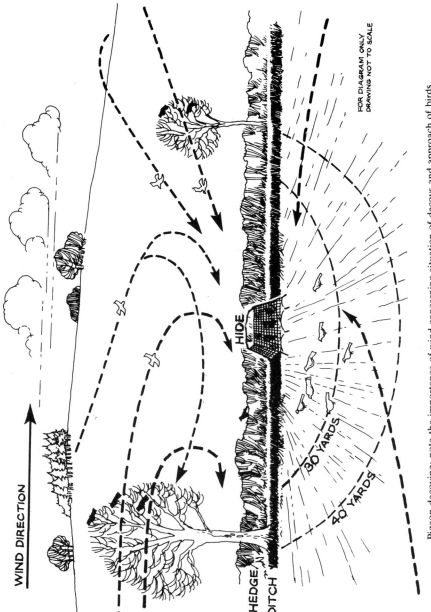

WIND DIRECTION

HIDE

HEDGE

DITCH

30 YARDS

40 YARDS

FOR DIAGRAM ONLY
DRAWING NOT TO SCALE

Pigeon decoying: note the importance of wind concerning situation of decoys and approach of birds

and any idea of shooting in there was quite out of the question. After a long, cold wait on one snowy February afternoon, the pigeons began returning from the fields to these woods. The first ten or fifteen minutes provided me with some very sporting shooting, and then I noticed that the birds following them were much higher, just out of effective shotgun range. As usually happens on these occasions, a small minority of the shooters continued to waste cartridge after cartridge on these high flying woodies, without so much as a feather to show for their foolishness.

The early shooting had served to warn the birds what to expect, but they had no intention of changing their roosting grounds. They merely relied on height to protect them from the barrage of shot, and once they were past the line of guns, they made for the plantations where they knew they were safe for the night.

Some of my happiest times spent in shooting pigeons coming to roost were during my school holidays, particularly around the festive season. I was very fortunate in that one of our neighbours, a retired businessman, enjoyed a shot, from time to time, yet was not sufficiently interested enough to rent a shoot of his own. He was, therefore, quite happy to accompany me into the woods at the rear of our house, where we had permission to shoot, most afternoons. I enjoyed far more success on these casual forays than ever I did at weekends, when the local guns were out in force. Two guns can shoot in a fair sized wood on several afternoons each week without causing undue disturbance to the flighting birds, and they are not likely to seek a change of roost at this relatively small provocation.

Apart from one or two specially organised woodpigeon shoots in aid of charity, when landowners and visiting guns co-operate to the full, I have seen little of the mass turn out of all the guns in the neighbourhood recently such as used to occur on those very popular Saturday afternoons, a few years ago. Perhaps it is a good thing in the long run. This type of shooting did little, on the whole, to reduce the woodpigeon population, merely disturbing them on one afternoon, and leaving them to ravage crops in peace for the remaining six days. Many people who had virtually no knowledge of guns or shooting, borrowed a weapon merely to join a comrade, who probably knew even less about it than they did themselves. Not only was game disturbed beyond all reason, but there was always the individual who was prepared to shoot a pheasant if he had the opportunity to do so, unobserved.

Pigeon-shooting during February and March still takes place, but nowadays it is usually organised by either the shooting syndicates or their gamekeepers, and guests are invited rather than an open invitation extended to all and sundry. The really keen shooting man should have little difficulty in obtaining shooting this way, for keepers are usually glad of bona fide guns during this time of the year, perhaps even asking them to partake in hare-drives once they have "proved" themselves.

Sometimes a pigeon-battue can provide the guns taking part with some fast and sporting shooting, but this is inclined to be the exception rather than the rule. If a man is keen to shoot pigeons regularly, in large numbers, then he must concentrate on becoming an expert in the use of decoys on fields where these birds are feeding regularly.

CHAPTER 9

Stoats and Weasles

THE DEADLY ENEMIES

Stoats and weasels are two of the deadliest enemies of game to be found on any shoot. They are the fiercest of all wild animals in the British Isles in spite of their size, and have been known, on occasions, to attack even a dog. Completely fearless, they are braver than the wildcat, that outlaw of the Scottish highlands.

The stoat is approximately 14 in. long, with reddish brown fur and white underparts. It is easily recognisable by the black tip on its tail. Its cousin, the weasel, however, is somewhat smaller, and has *no* black tip. They both hunt by scent, relying on rabbits for their staple diet, but they are equally as happy to devastate a chicken roost or a pheasant pen, lustfully slaughtering, like the fox, until not one of their victims remains alive.

Stoats and weasels, like rabbits and hares, do not integrate, and are inclined to have their own particular areas. They are a cunning

Stoat—black tip on tail. Weasel (below)—smaller

79

foe, and although the game-preserver, occasionally, may account for one with his gun, the major war will have to be waged with traps.

TRAPPING*

The modern humane traps are ideally suited to take these small creatures, but, like snaring, the quarry must be studied thoroughly before any real success can be obtained. The main point to bear in mind is that these creatures travel along hedgerows and stone walls, rather than across open country. If you have one or two stone walls on your shoot, then you can almost guarantee to trap a few here. I remember, as a boy, having a weasel take up residence in our rockery for some weeks during a spell of hard weather. We used to throw scraps of meat out for it, but its antics in enticing the local bird population within its reach, were the most interesting

Fenn trap being set alongside a barn for stoats

Photo: Lance Smith

NB: Under the *Wildlife and Countryside Act 1981,* it is illegal to take hedgehogs, wildcats, polecats, and pine-martens in either traps or snares.

feature of all. It would gambol about, performing all sorts of acrobatics, surrounded by a dozen or more sparrows. However, when I could see that it was manœuvring itself into a position whereby it would be able to grab the nearest one, I would bang loudly on the window, and bring the performance to an abrupt end.

I remember the first stoat which I trapped in my very early days of game-preservation. As an experiment, I dug a small trench about 18 in. long by 6 in. deep. On top of this I placed a wooden board which I covered with undergrowth, making a small, underground tunnel. Into this I pushed a conventional ''nipper'' rat-trap (no bait), completely uncovered. Nobody was more surprised than myself when, on looking at my tunnel the following day, I discovered that I had caught a fully grown stoat. Of course, it was sheer luck, but, nevertheless, it served as an early encouragement in my trapping career.

Stoats and weasels cannot resist entering a tunnel. Their curiosity makes them investigate any opening where they can see daylight at the other end. No bait is necessary, but it is advisable to cover the trap lightly with dead leaves. Care should also be taken to see that no scent remains on the trap. I usually bury new traps in the ground for a few days, or, when re-setting those currently in use, I wear gloves.

The more traps one has set, the greater number of catches one can expect, but, of course, it means a larger task when inspecting these tunnels. They should be looked at daily, preferably morning and evening if time permits. Seldom will even the most carefully set trap kill its victim outright every time, and any suffering must be reduced to an absolute minimum.

Tunnels for traps can easily be made at home, and, by doing this, much time will be saved in field and covert. Three pieces of wood nailed together, about 2 ft. long by 6 in. high, should suffice. A coat of green paint will blend them into their natural background, but they should be allowed to ''weather'' before being taken on to the shoot, for even the most curious stoat or weasel will regard fresh paint with suspicion. You have now made a simple tunnel in which to set your trap. You have a hedgerow or stone wall at your disposal, yet there are still one or two points to bear in mind. First, a slight indentation, scraped in the ground with a trowel, will settle the trap neatly at ground level. However, your trap must be secured with strong wire to either a nearby tree, post, or peg, otherwise that victim which is not killed outright will drag it off into the undergrowth, where it will die a lingering death. The wire should run under the side of the tunnel, and not out of one of the entrances, where it might obstruct the passage of the intended victim.

There is still one other thing you must do, though, before you leave your trap to its own devices for the next few hours. The most important aspect of trapping is to see that you only catch that creature for which your trap is intended. You don't want to arrive next morning, and discover that a pheasant, which you can ill-afford to spare, has foraged into your tunnel. Therefore, the insertion of a couple of strong wooden pegs, or branches, a few

Gin trap set. Now illegal

inches apart at either entrance, will restrict the passage of larger birds or beasts. Although you are principally out to reduce the stoat or weasel population on your land, there are other species of vermin which you will be pleased to account for in these same traps. Rats and grey-squirrels too, will be taken in this way, and it is gratifying to know that for every head killed, a possible brood of pheasant or partridge chicks may have been saved.

WEASELS CARRYING YOUNG

I had an experience with weasels one summer evening, several years ago, which proved something to me about which I had only, hitherto, read. I was seated in the undergrowth on the edge of a small spinney, hoping for a shot at a rabbit during the course of the evening. I had been there about half an hour when a movement in the long grass, about ten yards away, caught my eye. I watched closely, and then I saw a small head appear, and look around in a vigilant manner. It was a weasel. I did not hesitate, and a charge of No. 5 shot decapitated the fierce little mammal instantly. As I stood up to look at it, I was unprepared for the scene which lay before me. Lying dead, alongside the headless body of the adult weasel, was a youngster of the species, hairless, and no more than an inch in length. The significance of this did not dawn upon me until I turned away, and noticed something else, less than two yards from me. There, huddled on the ground, wriggling together for warmth, lay three more baby weasels!

There could be no doubt that the female weasel had been in the act of moving her four youngsters, possibly to a place of greater safety, following some disturbance. However, ardent game preserver as I was, I simply could not be so heartless as to grind these helpless creatures into oblivion with the heel of my boot. I debated with myself, seeking a solution to my dilemma, for to have left them where they were would have been equally as cruel.

Finally, I picked up all three of them, wrapped them in my handkerchief, and set off for home. I only wish that the story had a happy ending, but this was not to be. I had almost reached home, when a neighbouring boy of about twelve years of age, crossed over the road to speak to me. He was full of curiosity, realising only too well that I was attempting to hide something. Finally, I showed him the three young weasels, now content in the warmth of my handkerchief. When my young friend saw them, his eyes widened in amazement, and he pleaded with me to give them to him, in order that he might attempt to rear them. Seeing a way in which to relieve myself of the burden of my charges, I handed them over to him.

Alas, he disobeyed every instruction which I gave him concerning their welfare, and, wishing to hide them from his parents, for the time being, at any rate, he shut them in the sewing-machine for the night! It was not long, however, before the family cat devised a way of getting at them, and that was the end of what might have proved an interesting experiment.

POLECATS

We cannot leave the subject of stoats and weasels without mentioning another distant relative of their's—the polecat. Polecats are becoming increasingly more common in the British Isles, particularly in parts of Wales, although they are seldom seen in their natural surroundings except by those whose work takes them into the more remote hilly and thickly afforested areas. Much larger than either the stoat or weasel, they, too, are a nocturnal hunter.

A short time ago, whilst inspecting my network of tunnel-traps, I was amazed to find the structure overturned, the strong wire snapped, and the trap itself missing. There was evidence of much threshing about in the immediate vicinity, and I wondered what creature had managed to break the steel wire. The trail was not hard to follow, and a hundred yards or so further on, I came upon a fully grown polecat, the trap on one of its front legs, caught up in the briars. It could not have been trapped for long, I am grateful to say, for the brambles showed little signs of a struggle. I despatched it at once, and then set about finding whence it had come. Eventually, I discovered its lair at the base of a large oak tree. I am inclined to think that the hole leading down to the massive roots had been made long before, and this nomad of the hills had merely renovated it. I never saw any signs of its mate, and, to this day, I have not come across another polecat on my shoot. I am, indeed, sorry that it met such an untimely end, for, bloodthirsty as these animals are, I feel sure that I could have accommodated one on my 600 acres. Obviously, in areas where they are to be found in abundance, some sort of control has to be enforced, yet they are such fascinating creatures that the true lover of our countryside would not wish to see them bordering on extinction.

A gamekeeper friend of mine, then living only a couple of miles from my present shoot, had the same experience of catching a polecat in one of his tunnel-traps. Again, it was caught by one leg, but, instead of despatching it, he managed to transfer it to a sack, with the aid of a pair of thick leather gloves. Taking it home with him, he locked it in one of his sheds, leaving it an ample supply of food and water. It did not appear to be badly hurt, the jaws of the humane-trap merely bruising, whereas the teeth of a gin-trap would have virtually severed the limb. The leg was in no way broken. Each morning when my friend visited the shed, the polecat would dart behind boxes and various impedimenta, in order to hide from him. On the fourth morning, however, he decided to let it go free, for he judged that its wounds were sufficiently healed to enable it to obtain a living in the wild. On opening the door, though, he was dismayed to see it lying dead on the floor. We are both convinced that it was not the effects of the trap which had killed it. It had died pining for its freedom.

Stoats and weasels can, of course, be beneficial to a shoot in some ways. They will help to keep down the rats and mice, and stop the rabbit population from getting out of control. It is always a question of trying to maintain the balance of nature, something which is very difficult, nowadays.

Traps are best moved from time to time. Even the favourite ''killing'' place will eventually be known to the vermin on a shoot.

Perhaps they will have seen a relative perish there, and instinct warns them to avoid it. It is a good idea to re-site a couple of traps every week, unless a particular one is killing well, and then it should be left where it is, until, eventually, it is empty each day. A light setting is important for regular catching, and traps should be sprung a couple of times each week to prevent rust from jamming the action.

The young game-preserver will sometimes be misled into thinking that he has accounted for all his ground vermin simply because his traps are not catching, even after constantly changing their position. He must, remember, though, that tunnel-trapping is not constant throughout the year. The highest number of catches (it is always worth keeping a record) are invariably made during a spell of hard weather. However, it is a good idea to examine the corpse of any bird or beast found in field or covert. That tell-tale bite at the base of a rabbit's neck means only one thing—you've still got stoats and weasels on your shoot!

CHAPTER 10

The Crow Family

PREDATORS OF EGGS AND CHICKS

The Corvine Tribe; Carrion Crow, Hoodie Crow (Scotland), Rook, Jackdaw, Raven, Magpie, Jay, are most dangerous on the shoot during the nesting season. They have possibly the sharpest eyesight of all birds, flying slowly enough so that they are unlikely to miss that carefully concealed partridge or pheasant's nest. The game-preserver must wage war upon them throughout the whole year, the gun being his chief weapon.

CARRION CROW

The carrion crow is surely the worst villain of all around the game preserves. He is identified from his nearest cousins, the rook and the jackdaw, by the absence of white skin on the bill. A killer in black, he shows no mercy and is the curse of all wild birds, plundering eggs and fledglings of songbirds and gamebirds alike. He is a solitary bird, mostly seen either singly or in pairs, and never congregates in noisy colonies like the other corvines.

The rifle is the best weapon for waging war on the carrion crow at nesting time when it is of particular concern not to disturb sitting partridges and pheasants with a shotgun. Yet, stealth and perseverance are necessary if we are to come to terms with our enemy.

April is the crucial time for destroying any crows nesting on the preserves, but success is paramount, for a carrion crow driven from her nest will seek a more secluded place to rear a second brood, and, in all probability, will return with them to plunder as soon as they are old enough to fly, taking her revenge for your unsuccessful attempt to kill her.

Firstly the nest must be found, as unobtrusively as possible. The hen bird will depart at your approach, gliding silently away, and unless fired at she will undoubtedly return. Let her go, and once she is out of sight you must conceal yourself in the vicinity of the nest. Your task will be made that much harder if spring has come early and there is an abundance of foliage. You must pick your spot with regard to concealment as well as vision. There is no point in making yourself virtually invisible beneath the tree if you cannot see the nest. Usually the trees in question are tall, lone trees bordering a field, and you must take advantage of any undergrowth available.

As with jays and magpies, camouflage is essential, and you must keep perfectly still at all times. Just because your quarry is not in sight does not mean that she is not watching from afar, and there are few birds to equal the eyesight of the carrion crow. Wear a hat, and keep the brim pulled down to hide the whiteness of your face. Hold your weapon so that the minimum movement is necessary to train it on the crow once she alights on the nest.

Another ploy, an old ruse that seems to work time and time again, is for you to approach the tree in question with a companion, and once the bird has flown he walks away and you stay behind. Corvines, it appears, are not able to count, and once convinced that the intruders have left she will return.

The length of time that carrion crows remain absent from a nest, once disturbed, varies. There are instances of them having stayed away for several hours without apparently having jeopardised the fertility of the eggs. Often they will wait for dusk if they are put off in the evening, and although the darkness will help you to remain unseen it will also make shooting that much more difficult.

Consequently, it is of great importance, if possible, to situate yourself so that you are facing in a westerly direction and you will have a silhouette to shoot at. The moment she drops on to the nest, shoot her, because once she settles down on the eggs your opportunity will have been lost. A head shot must be your aim.

After a lengthy wait, when dusk is turning to darkness, and you are almost despairing, do not panic and hurry your shot at the last second. It is likely that you will not hear the bird's approach if she comes in from behind you, and the first you will be aware of her presence is when she alights on the edge of the nest.

MAGPIE

Most of us are familiar with the harsh chattering of the magpie, so different from the screeching of the jay, as we walk through some hitherto quiet tract of countryside. Perhaps we shall be fortunate enough to catch a glimpse of this attractive long–tailed black and white bird as it streaks for the nearest cover and then proceeds to taunt and insult us incessantly.

The magpie has increased in numbers considerably in all parts of Great Britain during the last few years. Handsome, yet so utterly ruthless, it is the arch–enemy of all conservationists and songbirds. Its eyesight is unrivalled, and it has the patience to watch and wait for hours in silence until it has located the nest of a sitting bird. Eggs are its favourite diet, and it will hunt systematically through fields and woods with an insatiable appetite.

Magpies are regularly seen on tracts of common land. This is not due, as may fondly be supposed, to a particular food to be found in these places but rather because the birds find immunity here from those engaged upon vermin control. Gamekeepers realise only too well the danger to which their young pheasants and partridges are exposed, and often magpies will occupy adjoining land where they cannot be pursued.

For the remainder of the year the magpie will be content to feed upon worms, insects and any grain which it might find. The author has counted as many as twenty feeding in a flock on a field of stubble. Between July and March it is relatively harmless to the countryside, and is an excellent sentry, raising the alarm for all fur and feather at the first sign of danger.

However, the magpie is far from being a shy bird. It may vanish into a nearby thicket and mock you unseen, but in suburban areas its audacity is unequalled except perhaps by its cousin, the jackdaw.

The magpie is a thief by nature and reputation. We cannot exclude it as the possible culprit whenever something bright and shiny goes missing. On many occasions it has ventured in through open windows, attracted by something that glitters and has caught its eye. Something light may be lost forever, but I remember some years ago when various items of dining room cutlery were discovered lying on the lawn outside. It happened during warm weather when the window was open, and I feel sure that had these knives, forks and spoons been lighter then they would have been taken back to the nest.

As mentioned before, songbirds live in terror of the marauding magpie. Even within the confines of a suburban garden they are not free from its plunderings, and all too often the urban dweller is inclined to blame a cat for the ravaged nest. It is a shame, indeed, that such a handsome bird has these characteristics. In many ways the magpie is far worse than the rest of its corvine relations because it confines its attentions to a particular area and works systematically. The carrion crow will fly for miles in search of the same prey, but often it will overlook the hedgerows and copses, and will not venture near human habitation. Not so the magpie. This bird will explore every inch of a privet hedgerow, and is cunning enough to take up a stance near an ornamental birdbath or birdtable and note the places to which the songbirds return.

The magpie's own nest is a domed structure with one entrance. A favourite nesting place is in a hawthorn bush, well concealed and uninviting to the birds'-nester. However, it, too, has its enemies. Owls and hawks will kill mercilessly, particularly the sparrow-hawk which is quite capable of striking its prey down whilst in flight. Nothing is so cruel as Nature herself in her efforts to maintain a balance.

Often jays and magpies are found sharing a comparatively small tract of countryside, but even when this happens they maintain their own territorial rights. They tolerate each other, but do not integrate. Their respective alarm notes can be heard once we trespass into their common domain. Once we have passed by, the search for eggs and fledglings will begin again.

WAGING WAR ON JAYS AND MAGPIES
The jay and the magpie are probably the most difficult of all species of vermin to come to terms with in thick woodland. They mock the keeper from a distance of only a few yards, screened from his view by thick foliage. With a shotgun he will only get one chance, hit or miss. At the sound of the first shot these colourful wicked birds will flit silently away to seek sanctuary in some other wood, perhaps in some place where they cannot be pursued. In such thick cover a rifle would be exceedingly dangerous and only the airgun will permit safe shooting. Nevertheless, we still have to lure these jays and magpies to a place where they can be seen and shot.

THE USE OF AN AIRGUN IN DENSE THICKETS
A small clearing in a dense wood is ideal for our purpose, but simply to walk in there in the middle of the day is no good. Our position will be noted by these corvines and we shall hear their taunting chorus for the rest of the day without catching sight of them. Thus, it is essential to be in position by first light. If a hide is necessary then it must be built a few days beforehand so that the birds become used to it, but generally in a place of this nature there is ample natural cover.

All the camouflage tactics used for pigeon or crow decoying must be employed, and as well as clothing that blends in with the undergrowth, a face mask is essential. There are some very good jay and magpie decoys on the market which, when used in conjunction with a rubber owl, are doubly effective. The author once used a stuffed golden eagle and Arctic snow owl with very good results, but the only snag with these was that they could not be used in damp weather.

A usually successful ploy is to use a handful of crock eggs, and make up a nest in the grass which can be seen easily from the surrounding trees. Better still would be some infertile eggs which can easily be obtained from most farms during the hatching season. A couple of shells can be broken in order to display a tempting yoke. These corvines are concerned with feeding once dawn has broken and are more inclined to be decoyed into a meal than a session of 'owl-baiting'. The scene is set. You are in your hide, dawn is breaking, and the 'nest' is set up beneath a tree which gives you the greatest vision. Before long you will hear the screeching of a jay or the chattering of a magpie. A point worth remembering is that jays and magpies, although occupying the same stretch of woodland, are territorial birds and you will seldom decoy both species together. You must determine which birds frequent this part of the wood and decoy accordingly. Possibly you will be concentrating on jays in which case it will be a mistake to put out a magpie decoy, for its rivals will merely mock it from cover. Personally, I think eggs alone are sufficient, and you may well end up with a mixed bag by mid-morning, including crows and grey squirrels!

Pick your shots, take your time, and shoot birds which you are reasonably certain of killing, either in the trees or at the decoy nest. Those which are missed will remember your ruse for a few days afterwards, and your luck will be in if single birds continue to appear. In all probability you will be shooting at a range of no more than 10 yards (9.14 m), and your quarry will present a much larger target than a bulls-eye at 25 yards (22.86 m). Aim for the head, and retrieve each dead bird. They can, of course, be set up as decoys by fixing a forked twig in the manner of a cradle, but any left lying around will only serve to warn the others.

In this manner it is possible to enjoy some excellent work as well as doing a very useful job on your shoot. The airgun, whether .177 or .22, will more than prove its worth during the close season.

THE CROW TRAP

This trap consists of a strong, wire-netting enclosure, and should be no less than 6 ft by 6 ft (1.83 m by 1.83 m) and the same height. In the centre of the roof, reaching down to within a couple of feet or so of the ground, is a tapered funnel constructed from the same mesh. There should also be a door through which the catches can be removed daily. The principle on which this works is that food (Crows will eat almost anything, and a couple of buckets of pigswill should suffice), is placed on the ground inside the enclosure. The Crows will drop down the funnel to it, but are unable to escape because their open wings, needed for take-off, prevent their obvious means of exit. Regular visits are necessary in order to remove these birds.

However, the Crow Trap is only worthwhile operating during severe weather. At other times the corvines will find ample food elsewhere. Another device which I employed at one time was a spring net-trap, very simple to operate, yet it only catches one bird at a time. Eggs being the ideal bait for carrion crows, I was constantly troubled with hedgehogs getting caught up in the net. It was sometimes a lengthy and difficult job unwinding the mesh which had become securely entwined around the creature's spines.

DECOYING AND CALLING

Decoying is the most effective method of waging war on crows throughout the year. Many years ago, as stated, I used a stuffed golden eagle which proved a sure 'draw' anywhere, the only snag being that I could not use it in wet weather. No other decoys or calls were necessary. Set up in a strategic position on the edge of a wood, the corvines would come from miles around to mob it. However, nothing lasts forever, and now I must content myself with the conventional rubber owl and crow decoys.

As with pigeons, the siting is important. The scene must look completely natural, and the concealment of the shooter is made that much more difficult on account of the quarry's excellent eyesight. The owl is best placed on a post, or branch of a tree, in ample view of circling crows. A crow decoy, placed a few yards away in a position of "investigation" will help to bring the birds in closer. In order to use a call with maximum efficiency, you must first listen to the various notes used by the crows themselves. The aggressive "growling" tone is suitable for this occasion. If, however, you are confronted with an apparently deserted countryside, and wish to entice a crow which you have heard in a neighbouring wood, use a long drawn-out "caw", repeated four times, at about two minute intervals, or more frequently if the bird

Rook

Carrion Crow

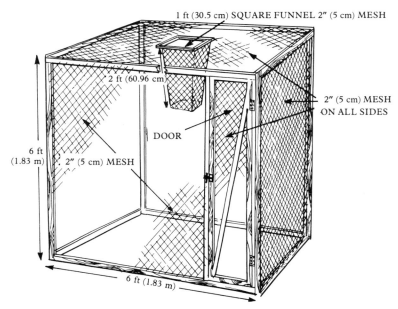

An easy-to-make crow and rook trap

begins answering your calling.

I once made some silhouette crow-decoys. They are the simplest of all to manufacture. All that is needed is to trace the outline of a dead crow on to a sheet of hardboard, cut it out, and paint it black, affixing a peg to the base so that it can easily be set up in a field. The thing to remember, when placing these out, is that although, basically, they must face into the wind, some deviation of positioning is necessary, otherwise, when a crow looks directly down on them they will disappear from his view for a few seconds, thereby creating suspicion. I have had moderate success with mine, but prefer the rubber variety in conjunction with my favourite stuffed golden eagle.

Jays and magpies can, of course, be decoyed in a similar fashion, replicas in rubber of both species being obtainable from specialist gunshops. However, these gaily coloured cousins of the crow are not to be found in such large numbers, and the man who is intent on sport, rather than game-preservation, will have to content himself with much smaller bags.

ROOK-SHOOTING

One of the delights of my boyhood was the annual rook-shoot which I used to attend with my father, on or around 12th May. This is something one rarely comes across today, and for no apparent reason. It used to be quite an occasion, with a lavish late supper laid on at the farmhouse afterwards, the party sometimes going on until the early hours of the morning.

As far as the actual shooting was concerned, those with .22 rifles positioned themselves in the rookery, accounting for the young birds in the branches, way above them, whilst the shotgun contingent on the outside dealt with the fliers, and the parent birds as they angrily flew to the protection of their young. All this was in the early days of my initiation with a .410, and I once shot six young rooks out of a total bag of 390! Nevertheless, there was an atmosphere which is lacking today, countrymen going about the task in hand with a quiet efficiency, a very necessary job being turned into a sporting occasion. Possibly, with the breaking up of the large estates, the new syndicate shoots are not interested in the rooks. This is something which they leave entirely to their gamekeeper, and if he cares to invite one or two friends along to help him, then that's up to him. I accepted an invitation from a keeper friend about five years ago, the result of which was a bag of 100 rooks shot by three of us. Had the particular syndicate decided to make a special occasion of it, and organise it properly, I have no doubt that 300 birds would have been accounted for.

RAVENS

One member of the corvine tribe which we must not overlook, whilst remembering at the same time that it is protected by law, is the raven. One will seldom see this, the largest of all the crow family, except in wooded hill country. Its numbers are so small, however, that it is unlikely to become a real menace to game. It is easily recognisable by its deep throated ''cronk'', and its size alone makes it easily distinguishable. However, the shepherds and hill-farmers do not regard it so favourably, for it frequently attacks newly born lambs if the ewe is incapable of defending her offspring. Nevertheless, our countryside would be that much poorer without the raven and, although it would be a sorry day for the game-preserver if its numbers increased to those of the crow, every effort should be made to preserve it wherever possible.

There is a raven living within a few miles of my former home, situated close to the industrial midlands. Yet it is not in its natural habitat, and it is only there because I brought it back from its native

Shropshire border hills. It is not a captive, though. It has been offered its freedom, but it has chosen to stay. In fact, the story of Drac the Raven is a very remarkable one.

Drac the Pet Raven

It was in early April that I first heard that the narrow strip of woodland adjoining my 600 acres of shooting rights in Shropshire was to be felled. I was dismayed for two reasons. This narrow belt of tall Scots pines provided a useful windbreak for my own place, and also, in the tallest tree of all, there had been, for as long as I could remember, a raven's nest. It was in the topmost branches of a massive fir tree, and every spring the birds could be seen, and heard, using it.

It was Bob Sanders who volunteered the terrific climb up to the nest, only a matter of a few days before cutting was due to start. I had mixed feelings about the whole prospect. I, personally, would not have scaled that tree, even had there been a bundle of five pound notes on the top. It was not only the height of the tree itself, which presented one with an awe-inspiring spectacle when contemplating the ascent, but the fact that it stood on the brink of a steep hillside going down to the valley below. A fall did not bear thinking about. On the other hand, I was curious to know if there was anything in the nest. It was a case of curiosity versus fear. I will never forget Bob's climb that warm April morning. I begged him not to go at the last moment, but he insisted, and I think the watching was worse than the actual climbing. It seemed an eternity as he worked his way slowly and painfully, branch by branch, towards the top. For some time I could not bear to watch, but when he shouted that he was almost there, I forced myself to look upwards.

The raven's nest was fully four feet across, built on three branches, and situated so that even the fiercest of gales could not get a grip on it. Each year, the pair of birds which decided to use it, renovated it, and possibly it had been in use for twenty years or more.

As Bob's head came level with the top of this masterpiece of corvine construction, there was a startled "cronk", and a flapping of wings. He recoiled, holding on for dear life, as a young raven landed on the branch above him. For a few seconds it perched there, before attempting to take wing. However, it had not yet gained full power of flight, and, instead, came fluttering down, to land in the grass, a few feet from me. Before it could recover from its surprise, I had thrown my jacket over it, and once in darkness, it made no attempt to struggle. It was with tremendous relief that

I saw Bob step down.

The problem now was what to do with our unexpected capture. We could not leave him at the mercy of the foxes and buzzards, and although the parent birds were circling high above us, mere specks in the sky, calling angrily, I could not see how they would be able to help their offspring. There was only one answer to the problem. We should have to take him home with us. We borrowed a large carton from one of the nearby hill-farms and, with some difficulty, for his razor-sharp beak presented a constant menace, we managed to get him into it. Once inside, he became quiet again, and within a couple of hours he was back at Bob's home in Lichfield.

The bird was Bob's, for it was he who had made the death-defying climb, and he was thrilled at the prospect of an unusual pet, even though he was prepared to release the raven when it attained full use of its wings. He set to work without delay, and quickly constructed a large aviary, bigger and better than most zoos would have used for this purpose. Drac, as he christened the raven, soon became accustomed to his new surroundings, and captivity did not appear to bother him in the least.

A few weeks later, the question of Drac's freedom arose, but he settled this problem for himself. The aviary door was one day left ajar after feeding time, and when my friend returned, some hours later, the raven had flown. Bob was quite upset about it, even though he realised it was for the best. However, Drac was not to be got rid of quite as easily as that. Reports came in a couple of days later about a raven in the vicinity of Lichfield Cathedral, a mere quarter of a mile away. It was feeding at the bird-table in the Dean's garden, and spending the rest of its time pecking the mortar out of the spires, and generally fouling the outside of the building. It was a cause for concern to the Dean and Chapter, but Bob quickly came to the rescue.

Strangely enough, Drac almost welcomed Bob when he appeared on the Dean's lawn one morning, during feeding time, and, with surprisingly little trouble, the bird was soon transferred back to his aviary home. He now appeared to show no inclination to escape at all, and Bob decided that if he was happy that way, he would keep him indefinitely.

What a character Drac turned out to be! I had heard stories of ravens kept in captivity before, and had always regarded them as mostly fiction, but I am now convinced how human these birds can become. Within months Drac had learned to talk, and was constantly uttering such phrases as "Drac's a good boy".

95

As for the ravens' home in that small belt of fir trees, it exists no more. Within a few days of our visit, every tree in that wood had been felled. However, it was not the end of the ravens in the area, for, the following spring, a pair built a nest in the tall larch trees in the valley below, and reared a pair of young successfully. The following year the same thing happened again. I was very pleased that, in spite of progress in modern forestry and farming methods, the gutteral "cronks" of Drac's relatives were still to be heard in the surrounding hills and valleys.

CHAPTER 11

Hawks

A PROTECTED SPECIES

Nowadays every species of hawk in Britain is protected by law. The sparrow-hawk was the last one to be afforded immunity from ruthless game-preservers. Indeed, it was the only way to save these predators from extinction. Myxamatosis deprived them of their staple diet more than twenty years ago. They had to adapt themselves to a new way of life, hunting wood-pigeons instead of rabbits, which is not an easy task for the slow-flying buzzard. Yet,

Sparrow Hawk

they survived, as did the conies, and now, at long last, the balance is being restored.

First, we must examine the question of hawks in relation to game-preservation. How much harm do they actually do? I am of the opinion that they are not nearly so detrimental to game-birds as we are inclined to think, an out-dated belief which is a relic of the last generation. The sparrow-hawk, for instance, is probably the worst of the lot. If he knows where to find pheasants, he will go after them. Yet, so low did the numbers of this bird of prey dwindle, that if the survivors had lived entirely on a diet of pheasant and partridge it would have made very little difference to the overall game population. Rogue as he is, the sparrow-hawk, then, will rarely trouble us.

The kestrel is the gentlest of the hawks, confining its attentions mostly to field-mice and moles. It is often seen in the vicinity of main roads, awaiting the corpses of small birds which have been killed by the speeding traffic. I have, though, personally seen it making off with a young pheasant chick from the keeper's rearing field. An odd instance, certainly, and since today most game-rearing is carried out in enclosed pens, as opposed to the 'open-field' system, then the kestrel will trouble us little. By the time the poults are turned into the wild, they will be immune to the attacks of so small a bird.

We must not disregard owls when talking of birds of prey. They are similar to the kestrel in their outlook, preferring a diet of mice and rats, with a game chick as a very occasional tit-bit. The only time when they are a real nuisance is when they frequent a wood where one's hand-reared pheasant poults are just learning to roost in the trees. Their presence will upset the birds, and often they will present Reynard with an easy meal by causing them to roost on the ground.

KITES

I once saw a kite passing over my Forestry Commission shoot in the Shropshire/Welsh border hills. It happened one sunny April morning, and so close was I to this bird that there could be no possible case of mistaken identity. I watched it for about ten minutes, until finally it was lost to sight, heading gracefully in the direction of the Long Mynd. Why and whence had it come? It was about this time that the massive trees in the Valley of the Kites, in Wales, were felled. The birds were dispersed, and sought out new homes in various parts of the country. Mine was not the only report of one such homeless kite in search of fresh territory. How I wish that it had chosen my own woodlands. However, I never saw it again.

CHANGE OF ATTITUDE BY GAMEKEEPERS

At one time a gamekeeper's maxim was, 'if it's got a hooked beak—kill it!' This, indeed, was a narrow-minded attitude, working on the principle that the particular bird might not kill one's game, but if it was dead, it certainly couldn't! One story which springs to mind, concerning this attitude towards our birds of prey, took place when I was attempting to decoy crows with my stuffed golden eagle, as I have mentioned elsewhere. I had 'Goldie' situated in a grass field on the afternoon in question, close to a spinney where I had built my hide. It was one of those days when there did not seem to be a crow in the vicinity, and suddenly I noticed two men creeping stealthily alongside the hedgerow on the opposite side of the field. I saw that one had a long stick in his hand, and there was no doubt whatsoever, that they had mistaken my decoy for a live bird. I decided to remain hidden, and to see what they were going to do. On and on they crept, until, finally, they were less than five yards from Goldie, and obviously very puzzled. Then, the man with the stick raised it above his head, preparatory to striking, and only my timely shout prevented Goldie from being reduced to a heap of feathers and sawdust. Perhaps they had envisaged stunning an already wounded bird, and selling it somewhere for a high price, or, maybe, they just had the urge to kill! Whatever their reasons, such actions will not help birds of prey to increase to their former numbers.

BUZZARDS

The buzzard is mostly only to be found in hilly wooded areas, like the raven, and although these two species are deadly enemies, they often live in fairly close proximity without interfering with each other unduly. The buzzard will sit for hours in a tree, perfectly camouflaged, waiting patiently until a young rabbit wanders unsuspectingly below, when he will drop on to it. Perhaps the odd pheasant poult will perish in this way, but one cannot condemn this majestic predator for taking advantage of such a situation. There is no finer sight than the buzzard, soaring effortlessly in wild mountainous country, its ragged, moth-like wings scarcely moving. It is reminiscent of its larger cousin, the golden eagle, in many ways.

Buzzard in flight. Note ragged, moth-like wings

A BUZZARD IN CAPTIVITY

Once I 'condemned' a buzzard to a life of captivity, but, in so doing, I undoubtedly saved its life.

It was a warm spring afternoon as John and I strolled through the thick Forestry Commission plantations in the Shropshire/ Welsh border hills. We were patrolling the boundaries of my 600 acres of shooting, in a casual sort of way, enjoying the fresh air and scenery, and looking for nothing in particular, although we had our guns with us in case the odd chance of a shot at vermin presented itself. Remus, my yellow labrador, panted at my heels, and seemed to know that this was strictly a 'close-season' outing for him. Two buzzards were circling far above us, and from the valley below a raven croaked. There was not a breath of wind, and it would have been almost a sacrilege to have fired a shot, and disturbed such an aura of peace and tranquility.

Suddenly, Remus put his nose to the ground, and began to move swiftly ahead of us. Thinking that he might have picked up the scent of a nesting hen pheasant, I called him to heel, but for once my order went completely unheeded. Instead, he broke into a run, and with a feeling of misgiving I saw him leave the woodlands and head down the slopes of a small valley, about three hundred yards away. We hurried in pursuit, but before we reached the wooded hillside, there was a sharp yelp of canine pain, and a couple of minutes or so later Remus rejoined us, his tail between his legs, and looking very sorry for himself. There was a scratch on the tip of his nose, and I was curious to discover what type of animal it was that had attacked him.

We began to descend the side of the valley, and this time Remus was more than content to remain at heel. The undergrowth was dense, and I was not very hopeful of discovering the creature we sought. Eventually, we arrived at the banks of the small stream which wound its way along the bottom, and then I saw the object of our search. It was a large buzzard, and it rested its back against the trunk of an oak tree, which stood on the water's edge, spitting and clawing in defiance. It was obvious that one wing was broken, and there is some cause for speculation as to how it had met with this misfortune. Possibly it had been engaged in battle with either a rival buzzard or a raven, or else some trigger-happy flockmaster had taken a shot at it on the lambing fields. Whatever the reason, I was now faced with the problem of either despatching it or attempting to remove it to a place of safety. It would have been heartless to have merely left it where it was, at the mercy of prowling foxes, once darkness fell.

I decided to try to capture it alive, a somewhat risky procedure considering its present temperament, and slashing talons. However, I found a dead branch, about four feet long, and with the aid of this I managed to knock the bird backwards into the water. The stream was about eighteen inches deep at that point, and once the buzzard was in it he was forced to spread his wings in order to remain afloat. The first part of my plan had succeeded, and now I had to chance the second. I leaned over and picked the spluttering bird, up, taking care to hold it by the extremity of its wing tips, and keep it well away from my face.

It was unable to reach me with either claws or beak, but I understood, at that moment, the old saying of having a "tiger by the tail". I then instructed John to remove my hat from my head, and drop it over the struggling bird. The moment this was accomplished, and the buzzard was in darkness, its struggles ceased, and it was a fairly simple matter to fold its wings, and drop it into the closed compartment of my game-bag.

Less than an hour later we were on the first stage of our 70-mile journey back to the industrial midlands in my Land Rover. The

101

bag containing the wounded buzzard lay on one of the rear seats. There was not a sign of life from it, not even a movement of the canvas when Remus sniffed at it from time to time. In fact, by the time we were half-way home, so concerned were we at the lack of sound from within the bag, that John decided to undo one of the straps in order to ascertain whether our captive was still alive. It

The buzzard was temporarily housed in a pheasant pen

transpired that it was very much in the land of the living, and my companion was fortunate in being swift enough to withdraw his hand before serious injury befell it!

My problem on arriving home was what to do with my newly acquired pet. Nobody that I knew would be willing to take it on. I housed it in a pheasant pen temporarily, but I would not be able to leave it there for long because I had a batch of day-old chicks ordered for the following week. I gave it a freshly killed rabbit and some water, but it refused either to eat or drink. All it would do was retire to the most secluded corner of the wire-netting run, where it adopted the same pose as when I had first seen it on the banks of the stream, hissing and spitting, its talons raised in a belligerent manner.

The following day brought about no change, and I decided that I would have to dispose of it somehow. I was reluctant to destroy it, and set about finding a good home for it. Consequently, I telephoned a small zoo which had recently opened, about twelve miles away. They were most enthusiastic about it, and offered to send someone to collect it on the following day.

The next morning a young student arrived from the zoo in a battered old Ford van, and, armed with a pair of large leather gauntlets, he had no difficulty in transferring it into a wicker-basket for easy transportation. Then he proceeded to tell me that it wasn't a buzzard, anyway. It was a kestrel, he said! I spent the next half hour giving him a brief lesson in elementary natural history!

One late summer evening, some months after my adventure with the buzzard, having nothing in particular to do, I decided to pay a visit to this interesting little zoo, mainly with the idea in mind of seeing how my bird was faring. I decided to go incognito, but having inspected the birds of prey area, without finding it, I approached the owner. No, the buzzard wasn't here any more, she informed me. It would have been cruel to have kept it in the small cages reserved for Kestrels and sparrow-hawks, and equally unwise to have housed it with a Crown Eagle. They knew of someone, in the next county, who kept a private menagerie and, as it happened, he already had one buzzard in a large outdoor aviary. His was a hen bird and mine was a cock, so fortune smiled on two very lonely birds of prey!

I never visited the place in question, but I have often spared a thought for the buzzard I found on that Spring afternoon. Is he content in his new surroundings, in the company of his mate, or does he still remember and yearn for the wildness of those beautiful border-hills? I shall never know, but I am satisfied that I did the best possible thing for him.

In case the reader should decide to try his hand at hawking, perhaps a brief mention of the type of equipment needed would not be amiss. A trained hawk costs in the region of several hundreds of pounds, so it is far cheaper to buy a young bird and train it yourself. In this case the beginner will be advised to seek expert advice for this would run to a book in itself, and a work on amateur gamekeeping does not lend itself to this subject in detail.

However, the basic equipment needed is as follows:

1. **Hawks can either be tethered to an outside perch or kept in a special hawkhouse. They are usually tethered to an arching bow-perch stuck in the ground.**
2. **Falcons are given a block perch or pedestal.**
3. **The Cadge is a portable square frame perch used for carrying several birds at a time in the field.**
4. **Jesses are leather leg straps six to eight inches long with a swivel and a leather leash.**
5. **Bells are fitted to legs, tail or neck of birds to assist in the location of a missing bird. However, there is also a small radio transmitter on the market which is fitted to the jess. A directional receiver gives several miles range.**

CHAPTER 12

Fox Control

Foxes are the most controversial of all vermin when it comes to control. Whatever method you adopt, you will be criticised by somebody, so you must decide from the moment that you sign the agreement, or lease, for your shooting rights, which side you are on. Somebody recently came up with the idea that you can have both foxes and pheasants living side by side, amicably on your shoot. Well, to be blunt, you can't! It is as simple as that, and you must make up your mind which you want.

There are three recognised methods of fox-control:

1. Hunting.
2. Shooting.
3. Snaring.

I once saw an advertisement offering a large cage which purported to catch foxes up on the shoot. I have no doubt that it would, if set in the appropriate place at the right time of year. Yet, it was a dear buy for the amateur game-preserver, requiring daily inspection, and if there is a large acreage to cover, then it will cost you more to reduce your foxes than to rear your pheasants!

SNARING*

First, let us take a look at *snaring*, undoubtedly the most efficient method of combating Reynard on his own territory. There is only one way to snare foxes on a weekend shoot, and I will endeavour to describe this method in detail. To begin with, you must find about fifty well-used fox-runs. On my own shoot this works out at about one run to every ten acres. Fix your snares in position, but do not set them up on the "props" yet. They are best left lying there for a fortnight or so, and Reynard will continue to use these same routes without suspicion.

If you are not living in close proximity to your shoot, you will

NB: Self-locking snares are now outlawed under the *Wildlife and Countryside Act 1981*. All free-running snares are required by law to be inspected at least once daily.

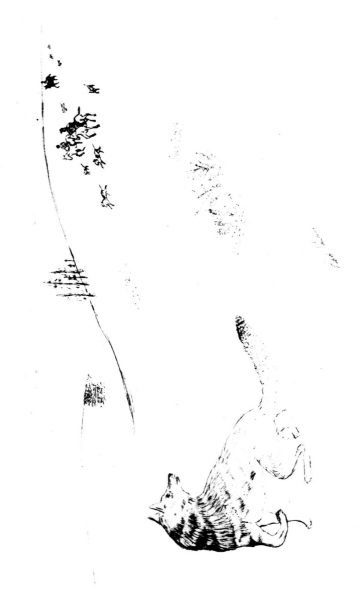

Fox and hounds. Hill foxes are inclined to be slightly more heavily built

need two consecutive free days. On Saturday, for example, go round your runs, and set the snares up in position, *using gloves* in order not to leave any scent for your wires will be set for one night only, and you want to give them every possible chance to catch in readiness for your inspection and removal on the following morning. I like the loop of my snare to be about four inches from the ground, depending, of course, on how dense the undergrowth is, as, in most cases, a fox will be travelling with his nose very close to the ground. I find that it is much easier to tie a snare to a nearby tree with strong wire, than to knock a separate stake in for each snare. Also, it is much more secure.

One very important factor concerning snaring, is to avoid carrying out your onslaught during a period of a full moon. Almost every fox that is snared is caught at night, and the moonlight will only serve to show up your wires, resulting in no catches, and a wasted journey.

As I have mentioned before, many people's hand will be against you, and great care must be taken to see that somebody else does not get a chance to find a fox in a snare which has not been recently inspected. I try to set all my snares out of sight of paths and rides, for they are not a pleasant thing for the casual walker to come up on, anyway.

I have a theory of my own about snaring, and this is that a fox can nearly always be caught in a wire set close to the carcase of another fox. My best example of this was when I caught a vixen one summer, and, leaving the corpse where it was, I snared five cubs and the old dog-fox nearby!

The best way of despatching a snared fox is to shoot it. I never begrudge the price of a cartridge, and it is a far more humane method than trying to bludgeon the animal to death with a fencing-stake. There is also the chance that, whilst you are attempting to club it, it may snap the wire and escape.

If a fox appears to be dead in the snare, make certain of this before attempting to remove the wire from around its neck. I was once very lucky to escape being badly bitten when I thought one was finished. If in doubt, give it a barrel.

I had a very strange catch in one of my snares once, namely a *bicycle* with no wheels! I looked a second time to make sure that I wasn't seeing things, but it was most certainly a bicycle. At that time I was having snares constantly stolen by some unknown person, and it was, no doubt, intended as a joke by this same offender. Possibly he had some peculiar fad against snaring foxes, and I am sorry that I never caught him thieving!

I have been asked, on several occasions, by various people, to catch them a fox-cub to rear as a pet. I have no intention of doing any such thing as I think it is unfair to both foxes and humans. When I was a small boy, a farmer's wife, near to where we lived, made a pet of a cub from a litter which her husband had dug out. They kept it for three years, and then, one day, it escaped. A few weeks later my father was on that same farm, shooting rabbits at harvest time, when he shot a fox which bolted out in front of the binder. The animal in question was found to be wearing a collar, and the farmer later identified it as his wife's lost pet. I think it would take centuries of domestic breeding before foxes became fully acclimatised to living in captivity, and I have no intention of encouraging these predators to be reared as pets.

Casual motorists, driving along the narrow lanes bordering my shoot, will stop, and gaze at my "vermin gibbet" just visible inside the first conifer thicket. They will see, hanging there, all species of vermin, including foxes. In many shooting circles, it is an unforgiveable crime to kill a fox, let alone hang it up as evidence of your deed. However, I view this differently. Since I have been killing foxes regularly, I have made some very good friends amongst the local farmers and shepherds. If they do not actually *see* the foxes which I have killed, they have only my word for it. I prefer to present them with the evidence. I know that one or two of them make special journeys up from the valleys below to inspect my line of vermin, and this affords them considerable pleasure. They know that at least those particular foxes will not be troubling them again.

If the casual observer takes an even closer look, he will see that none of the foxes on the line have tails. I have removed all these, not only as a means of keeping a tally, but to cure. They look superb hanging on the wall of one's study, or in a local public house.

Skinning a Brush

However, there is a definite art in skinning a fox's brush to perfection. A freshly killed fox is much easier to work on, rather than one which has been dead for two or three days. First, one must nick around the tail where it adjoins the body. Then, keeping one foot on the corpse to hold it down, peel the skin back slowly. The hardest job is getting it started. After the initial pull, it should peel off very easily. A stick of the of the same length as the brush should then be inserted inside it. Immediately upon returning home, remove this stick, pour white spirit liberally into the hole, and then replace the support. The hardest part is now completed, and the brush can be hung in a shed for several weeks, without further attention, until the curing process has been completed. It will now be soft and pliable, and ready for whatever purpose has been designed for it.

SHOOTING

We now come to the alternative method of controlling your fox population—by shooting. It has been hailed as the most humane method, far more so than hunting and snaring. Actually, it is the most cruel of all, unless carried out by an expert.

You can either organise a drive, inviting other guns, and a few beaters and dogs, or you can set out on a lone foray. The latter is likely to be more successful in the long run. Early morning or evening is the best time if you are a lone wolf, hoping to catch Reynard either as he is setting out on one of his nocturnal rambles, or as he returns. Your dog is best left at home, for the least scent available for your quarry, the better. A central vantage point is vital, either where rides adjoin, or perhaps by a woodland pool where he is in the habit of coming to drink. It is necessary to conceal oneself as if the sharp-eyed crow was the object of your attentions, allowing freedom of movement at the same time, for you will probably have to shoot quickly when a fox shows up. Try to site your position so that the wind is blowing from where you expect Reynard to come.

Only very heavy shot should be used, preferably BB or AAA. Anything larger may result in a complete miss for there is no pattern worth speaking of with SSG or SG. Thirty yards should be regarded as a maximum range, and the head should be the main target. I sometimes use a commercial rabbit call when I think there is a fox in the vicinity.

Organised Drives

Organised fox-drives may provide a congenial gathering for local farmers and shooting men, but, usually, they achieve little else. These are the occasions on which foxes escape wounded, and die a lingering death. One pellet alone is sufficient to cause gangrene in this animal, and there is usually somebody who cannot resist a shot at 60–70 yards!

However, if you do decide to organise a drive on your shoot, some forethought may well be to your advantage, as well as minimising suffering amongst the foxes. First, invite only reputable guns, but ascertain whether or not they are for or against shooting

One fox less

foxes. Otherwise, you will not only offend them, but earn yourself a dubious reputation at the same time. It is a good idea if you provide the cartridges. A few BBs, handed round out of your box of wildfowling cartridges, will ensure that large shot is used. After all, the removal of the foxes from your shoot will be well worth it, and if half a dozen shots are fired during the course of the drive, that will be all.

If beaters are unobtainable, then it will be as well to have half the company walking the ground towards the remainder, who are strategically placed. Great care must be taken, though, for if somebody is struck by a stray pellet, it could be far more serious than a No. 6 shot incurred whilst driving partridge or pheasants.

The walking guns must move slowly, allowing the dogs time to work, otherwise a fox may lie close, and then double back after the line has passed. The middle of the day is often a good time to drive foxes. Often they will be lying above ground, in dense undergrowth, and can be moved out reasonably easily. If you have a well-used fox-earth in your woods, then a terrier is an asset. However, ascertain beforehand that the dog has worked foxes before, for an inexperienced one can suffer terrible injuries if it manages to corner its quarry.

HUNTING

Finally, a word about fox-hunting. It is often advisable to allow the hounds to draw your shoot when permission is sought, providing it will in no way be detrimental to your game. February and March are the months when the least harm will be done, before nesting begins. It is inadvisable to oppose the hunt except when there is a reason for doing so. Who knows, they might even do you a favour and kill one of your foxes!

Whilst on the subject of hunting, it is the *least cruel* method of all, contrary to popular belief. The fox is almost invariably dead when the hounds finally rip it to pieces, its neck quickly broken by the initial encounter. However, that is as it may be, and I believe in allowing others to pursue their sport, unmolested, whilst I enjoy mine. We must learn to live side by side.

One final point to bear in mind whilst on the subject of depredations by foxes, is that Reynard will, undoubtedly, like the human murderer, return to the scene of his crime. If, one morning, you discover that a fox has found its way into your pheasant pen, don't immediately clear up the ravaged corpses in a fit of anger and depression. Instead, return at dusk with your gun, and take up a well-concealed position nearby. The chances are that, before morning, you will see your fox. I know a gamekeeper who was faced with a similar situation. He waited, patiently, until just before dawn the next morning, before he finally accounted for the culprit with a well-directed charge of BB. It had been well worth the long vigil, though.

Yet, we do not seek to exterminate the fox from our countryside. Indeed, it would not be the same without him, rogue as he is. We must merely control his numbers, in the most humane method possible, so that our efforts at rearing game are not entirely wasted.

CHAPTER 13

The Starling Menace

Starlings are not merely a curse which descends upon the game-preserver during the winter months. They are equally detrimental to agriculture and forestry, not to mention the amount of damage which they do in the towns and cities, whilst roosting on high buildings. Their incessant chattering can be heard above the roar of the rush-hour traffic.

MIGRANT BIRDS

Yet, these starlings are not home-bred birds. Mostly they come from the continent, and as far afield as the U.S.S.R., preferring the warmth of Britain, in its severest weather, to the devastating cold of the Russian steppes.

Their worst factor is the carrying of disease, such as foot-and-mouth, from one farm to another. Fields of winter-corn can be destroyed in a matter of days, and the ground fouled with the excrescence of these vile birds. Scavengers, like rats, I can find no redeeming feature in them. I read once of a professional wildfowler who used to fire his punt gun into the midst of these flocks, selling the carcases for 2d each in the market. This was at the turn of the century, though, but I doubt whether, even with today's world food-shortage, they would be regarded as edible.

Starling Roosts

Often, starlings will choose the same roost, winter after winter, and if it happens to be your pheasant covert, then you've really got a problem on your hands. Pheasants will not share a wood with starlings. Instead, they will seek quieter places, away from the nocturnal bad-tempered twitterings, and foul stench.

However, if the starlings in your wood are accessible, then with luck, you may be able to move them. Shooting is a pure waste of good cartridges. Pigeon-scarers and coloured flares will be far more effective. Great care must be taken, however, to see that you

113

do not set your wood on fire. Of course, you will have to disturb your roosting pheasants. They will be driven elsewhere for a week or two, but even this is better than having a wood permanently full of starlings.

You may not be so lucky, though. I remember a case where a large wood was cursed with vast flocks of migrant starlings, and their rhododendron stronghold was virtually inaccessible. Apart from the usual threat to the surrounding countryside, their presence was a dire peril to the community which drank from the underground reservoir beneath their roost. It was something which I shall remember for the rest of my life, and the fierce battles which we waged in an attempt to drive them away.

Starling Invasion
It was November when the starlings first arrived in the beautiful woodlands at the rear of our house. At first they were barely noticeable, a few flocks of migrant birds joining the resident ones as they flighted, to and fro to the fields, daily, to feed. Gradually, however, the numbers built up, and they made their presence known by their deafening chatter, as they jostled for roosting places in five acres of dense rhododendrons each night.

The starlings resembled hordes of locusts   Photo: Guy Smith

By the beginning of December they resembled a vast horde of locusts as they left the woods at first light, and returned at dusk. Their depredations were evident to any who cared to take a stroll in this enchanting tract of countryside. Larch trees, rhododendrons, and the ground beneath them, were all white with their droppings, seeming as if there had been a sudden overnight snowfall. The stench was putrifying, reaching the houses below when the wind was in that direction, cloying the nostrils, and bringing about a feeling of nausea.

At first, the inhabitants of the nearby village showed little interest in the starling army which had invaded their surroundings, merely choosing to exercise their dogs elsewhere. It was the local Waterworks Committee who first showed concern over the state of affairs, for they feared lest these scavengers might pollute the underground reservoir beneath their roost. Consequently, after a "crisis" meeting, a decision was reached, and it was decided to hold a series of shoots on three consecutive evenings. However, by the time the necessary arrangements had been completed, it was already April.

The Starling "War"

Troops had been engaged from a nearby barracks to fire explosive rockets into the circling flocks, whilst many of the shooting men in the area had been invited along, presented with a couple of boxes of cartridges each, and told to "fire at will". I well remember taking a muzzle-loading 14-bore with me, which I had acquired only the previous week, and adding a few devastating blasts to the constant barrage around me.

The starlings were not prepared to surrender their stronghold easily. They bunched together, resembling a gigantic swarm of bees, defied the concentrated fire for an hour or more, and finally dropped down into the safety of their rhododendrons under the cover of darkness. On the second evening, fewer birds returned to the woods as dusk closed in, and, on the third, the numbers were so small that the project was deemed to have been a complete success. Those who had participated in this "warfare" were cordially thanked for their services, and with the coming of summer the whole business was conveniently forgotten.

The following winter, there was no sign of the starlings returning, and we all firmly believed that these birds from Russia and the continent had made their home elsewhere. However, only a few days prior to Christmas, our woodlands suddenly became invaded, almost overnight, the contingents of starlings seemingly even more

GAMEKEEPING AND SHOOTING FOR AMATEURS

concentrated than in the previous winter. Within a matter of days, the whole area was inches deep in their foulings, and early January found the Waterworks Committee planning yet another campaign. The procedure was much the same as before, with explosive rockets and a large number of shotguns comprising the armaments to repel the enemy. Once again, I took along my antiquated muzzle-loader, together with a conventional breech-loader, for the former did not allow me the rapid fire so necessary in preventing the angry black clouds from gaining their sanctuary.

There was a different atmosphere about the shoots this time, however. The guns were less relaxed, perhaps the hard weather at the time lending a more business-like approach to the whole scheme. It was not just an outing with the gun, for everyone amongst us realised the seriousness involved, and the importance of moving the starlings away from the underground water-supply in the dead of winter.

For three nights the battle raged fiercely. The firing was incessant, rockets were exploding continually, and gun barrels became too hot to hold. Yet, each evening, as darkness fell, the tens of thousands of birds which had survived the vicious onslaught, dropped down to roost in the rhododendrons. Even on the third evening, the result was the same, and it was quite evident that this time we had not won.

It was estimated that each shoot had cost something in the region of £30, and the Waterworks Committee decided that further shooting, as well as being useless, was not possible as the finances allocated for this purpose had now been exhausted. Consequently, the starlings were left in peace, and they continued to enjoy immunity in these woodlands until mid-April, when all but the local-bred birds had departed for their own countries.

Much controversy has arisen concerning the success of the first series of shoots compared with the failure of the second. My own theory is that when the initial shooting took place, it was already April, and the starlings were preparing to leave. The disturbance may possibly have hastened their departure by a few days, but certainly it was not the main factor in driving them away. However, the second attempt was carried out in January when they had no incentive to leave. Thus, they doggedly refused to leave, stood firm and won their fight.

The starlings have never returned since. Obviously, they have found a more convenient winter roost, free from disturbance. I would not wish them on anyone, for they are a terrible curse to descend upon any area of peaceful countryside, transforming it into an area of concentrated desolation and filth, within a matter of days.

Of course, narcotics would probably be the answer to the starling problem, and the use of alpha-choralose would soon diminish concentrated flocks of the speckled menace. However, I hope that this method is never attempted, as it once was on woodpigeons. The effects would be too far-reaching, and many game-birds and songsters would die as a result. Instead, we must combat the starlings as we find the flocks, hoping that we can drive them to roost in those places where they can do the least amount of harm.

CHAPTER 14

Badgers

Since 25th January, 1974, it has been illegal to take or kill badgers without a special licence. This Act was long overdue, and perhaps now the much-persecuted Brock will at last be able to breed prolifically again. Too long has he been regarded as vermin by game-preservers who should have known better. Badger digging I can in no way condone. He is the most handsome and friendliest fellow of the woodlands, and fully deserves the legal immunity bestowed upon him.

"ROGUE" BADGERS

The badger is virtually harmless to game, his staple diet being young rabbits taken from nearby warrens. Occasionally, though, an old badger, no longer able to forage for his own food, will raid the coverts in search of hand-reared pheasant poults. It is this

Badger. Note the shortness of the legs

"rogue" which has earned his more active colleagues the title of "vermin". However, perhaps in this more enlightened age, gamekeepers, generally, will recognise him for his true worth, and not partake in illegal forays after him.

Yet, the badger can be ferocious at times. I recall, many years ago, an old gamekeeper setting forth with his gun, early one May morning, to wait by a sett which he knew was well used. It was not long before the boar emerged, less than thirty yards from him. Quickly, the keeper fired a No. 4 at its head. The animal whirled round, and caught the second barrel. Suddenly, it charged, and the frightened man took to his heels, running as fast as he could through the undergrowth. He could almost feel its powerful jaws closing upon his legs when the pursuit ended as abruptly as it had begun. The badger rolled over, stone dead, and lay at the feet of the breathless man! This, in itself, was a senseless killing, and served no purpose whatsoever.

Badgers are not a ferocious species, but they are a formidable foe if cornered. Of course, nowadays, one has no business cornering a badger, but where they are kept in captivity there is always the question of this arising. Accidents may happen, too, such as Brock stumbling unwittingly into a fox-snare, and then the unfortunate keeper has the unenviable job of releasing him.

The jaws are the most powerful amongst our native wild animals, and it is as well to consider the action to be taken if one day you discover a badger in one of your wires. Cutting the wire at its point of anchorage is nothing short of cruelty, for not only does the creature stand a chance of becoming caught up elsewhere, but the snare will cause untold suffering before he finally rids himself of it . . . if ever.

Assistance is essential if you are to avoid a nasty bite. So, having recruited a willing farmhand or some other such handy person, cut a large forked stick, preferably ash. Then, position yourself so that you can pin the struggling creature down by its neck, and whilst your companion attempts to hold it thus, cut the wire free of the badger, and then leap to safety! Badgers are usually only caught in badly set snares where the noose is lower than the height necessary to catch a fox. Snares should be set so that the wind does not dislodge them, thus making them a danger to the prowling badger.

THE SETT

I remember, as a boy, visiting a huge badger sett in the woods at the rear of our house. It consisted of roughly an acre of ground, amid some silver-birch trees, and I used to take a bag of fallen apples with me occasionally, depositing the damaged fruit outside the largest entrance, and then returning the following day to see whether or not my offering had disappeared. Almost invariably it had.

DOMESTICATED BADGERS

I am no more in favour of domesticating badgers than I am of foxes. Yet, the former seem quite at home in the company of humans. I remember seeing one once at a clay-pigeon shoot, of all places. Its owner, and his son, took it in turns to look after their pet whilst the other shot, and it did not appear to mind wearing a collar and chain. Of course, it had been taken from a sett when it was very young, and I have a shrewd suspicion that its parents were the victims of badger-diggers.

CLEANEST OF ALL WILD CREATURES

Brock is the cleanest of all wild creatures. Any careful observer at his place of habitation, will note the well-used track leading away from the main excavations. If he follows this, he will come upon an area amid the undergrowth where the droppings of this animal will be in evidence. This is the "toilet", for the badger, unlike the fox, will not dream of fouling his own quarters.

BADGER DISCOVERY

I think one of my proudest moments was on the day that I discovered a colony of badgers on my own shoot, in the Shropshire/Welsh border hills. Such pleasure did my discovery afford me, that I make no apology for relating the circumstances in this passage.

I had been two years in the Shropshire hills before I realised that I had badgers on my land. This may seem rather a naive statement, but, there again, one does not associate Brock with inhabitating an area of 600 or so acres of thickly planted Forestry Commission woods. Not for him these artificial woodlands, but rather the older woods, with long established setts, which had been the home of his father and his father before him.

It was during April, following one of those delightful falls of snow which frequently occur in these border hills at this time of year, enhancing the scenery, yet too slight and brief to be of any serious threat to the sheep farmers, that I first saw badger tracks along one of the narrow ridges. I followed them for possibly a quarter of a mile, until they finally turned into a dense thicket, and disappeared. I thought that perhaps it was just a beast of passage, traversing my land on its way down to some woods in the valleys below, and I thought little more about the incident.

Badger Wood

Then, one day, a flockmaster, with whom I paused to pass the time of day, mentioned the fact that once there had been a "badger wood" on my land. That had been in the days before the Forestry Commission had planted their Norwegian Spruce and Scots Pine, and changed the whole geographical structure of the locality. Yes, he remembered the small spinney on the far slopes of the hill. A few oak and beech trees, nothing much to look at, but a haven for badgers. They were seldom interfered with, for weekend visitors were a rarity in those days and, anyway, the inaccessibility of the setts was enough to deter all but the hardiest of hill-walkers. He sighed, lamenting the modern method of economic forestry, and all that it destroyed in its object purely to produce timber.

The following week found me on the eastern side of the hill, an area which I rarely had cause to visit, standing on the rough, man-made road, and surveying the deep green, tree-covered slopes above me. Suddenly, my heart leapt, for I saw something which I had not noticed previously, or rather the significance of which had not registered on my mind. There, about half way up the hillside, like a small island in an expanse of water, stood a group of a dozen or so massive oak and beech trees in the midst of the coniferous thickets. Was this the Badger Wood of old?

I determined there and then to visit this place in an attempt to discover if, indeed, it was the original home of the Brock in this part of the border hills. However, this was easier said than done, for apart from the steepness which would have rendered it a fairly difficult walk anyway, the whole slope was a mass of thick spruce, unbrashed, with no sign of a "fire-break". The journey would have to be undertaken by crawling up there on hands and knees, below the lowest branches, a task which I did not relish!

It was the stream which provided the solution to my problems as I stood there pondering on the difficulties which lay ahead of me. It most certainly had its source somewhere up there, and the Forestry Commission would hardly have planted young trees in its course. As it went gushing down to the valley below me, I determined to follow this water course from whence it flowed, hoping that it would lead me to within crawling distance of my destination.

Stooping low, for the branches of the trees on either side of this narrow rushing stream met overhead, I began the long climb,

121

walking against the current, the water almost up to the tops of my Wellington boots. The sunlight only penetrated through in places, and it was almost like twilight as I slowly began the ascent of the hillside. The stony, moss-covered bed of the stream provided a treacherous foothold, and the water was icy cold. At one point I paused to slake my thirst, for the going was hard, and never have I tasted purer water, so different from that which is piped to more civilised areas.

Another two hundred yards farther on, and the stream became narrower and narrower, until finally it disappeared altogether, or to be more precise, it went underground. However, the stony dry course still continued ahead of me, and I could only conclude that at some time or other the water had flowed above ground here also, perhaps reafforestation being responsible for its deviation.

My progress became increasingly more difficult now, until finally I was forced to crawl on my hands and knees. Had I not come so far, I should have abandoned the idea, and turned back there and then. However, I felt that I could not be too far away now, and a few minutes later my hopes were realised as I saw sunlight through the trees ahead of me.

It took me a couple of minutes or so to adjust myself to the brightness, after the gloom in which I had been for the past hour or so. As I gradually took in the scene before me, I felt a thrill, and a great sense of satisfaction, for I knew that I had been right after all. This was the old Badger Wood. There was no doubt at all about this, for the spinney, some half an acre in size, was a maze of setts, and mounds of freshly excavated earth, "toilet" runs and piles of dead leaves. Possibly, I was the first person to set foot there since the forestry workers had left.

I noticed a large, brick constructed, rectangular block standing on the far side of the clearing. It was about 10 ft. long by 5 ft. wide, and about 4 ft. high. On closer inspection I discovered that it was a type of reservoir, built many years ago to conserve the water as it ran down the slopes from above, possibly the only source of supply for the isolated cottages in the valley below. No doubt, this was when the course of the stream had been altered. Now this reservoir was forgotten, perhaps providing a steady flow of water for stock to drink from the "dingle" below, but otherwise of no use to mankind.

Badger 'Island'

This was not a wood, it was an island, remote from the rest of the countryside, and protected from outside interference by the almost impenetrable belts of fir plantations. Life went on there now as it had done for generations. Nothing stirred, and I felt almost guilty as though I was a trespasser. I could not help admiring the policy strictly adhered to by the Forestry Commission of leaving large trees such as this for the benefit of bird life principally. They are very thoughtful in this respect, realising the necessity of providing nesting sites for birds of prey such as the buzzard. In sparing these few trees they had also encouraged Brock to remain with them.

Finally, I dragged myself away, almost reluctant to leave and begin the long descent back to my own world. I knew that I was leaving something very worthwhile behind me, but I would come back again some day, if only to satisfy myself that no other intruder had found his way there.

It is such places as these which have been responsible for the continued survival of the badger throughout the years when almost every gamekeeper's hand has been against him.

CHAPTER 15

Stocking With Pheasants

HATCHING AND REARING

Contrary to popular belief, pheasants are not difficult to rear. However, before I discuss the methods suitable for rearing a brood on the back lawn it is advisable to have some knowledge of producing pheasants on a larger scale. The professional gamekeeper has two choices open to him. He can either adopt the "open-field" system, or else rear his birds in coops with wire run-outs attached. The former is not extensively used today, mostly because it requires a man constantly on duty in the rearing field. The broody hen is confined in a coop with a slatted front which allows the chicks to run freely in and out as they please. They learn to run back beneath her whenever she clucks in alarm, but, nevertheless, they are exposed to the threat of both winged and ground vermin.

Years ago, on almost every large estate, we should have seen rows of coops in the rearing-fields, chicks darting amidst the long grass like mice, and the gamekeeper in his hut boiling up the next feed, his gun close by in case a hawk should suddenly put in an appearance. Everything seemed much more natural and leisurely in spite of the burden of work and worry.

Nowadays, the scene has changed. Those same fields contain rows of pens, the chicks restricted in their foraging after insects. No longer can a hawk swoop on an unsuspecting week-old pheasant, and carry it away in a flash. Yet, although the need for constant vigilance has been reduced, the keeper has additional work. The pens must be moved daily on to fresh grass, and as the poults grow they resort to feather-pecking in their boredom. No longer does he have to boil and mix quantities of mash, though. Modern foods in pellet form contain all the vitamins necessary to growing birds. He has gained on the swings what he has lost on the roundabouts, to coin a much used phrase.

The choice of the rearing-field is important. It must not have had game or poultry on it for a minimum of three years, it must be reasonably level, and situated in a well-drained, dry place, on grass with plenty of seed. The more sunlight the birds get, the better.

The keeper catches up his stock birds immediately after the shooting season is over, penning them in the ratio of one cock to six hens. The hens begin laying in April, but often it is advisable to exchange a percentage of eggs with other estates in order to inject fresh blood into the existing stock.

Bantams make better foster-mothers than ordinary hens, but the acquisition of broodies today is a nightmare to every keeper. Modern poultry methods do not allow for broody hens, and his search leads him to remote farms and small-holdings where "free-range" is still practised. The broody must sit on dummy eggs for at least the first week, otherwise there is a grave risk that if she loses her broodiness she will either smash the eggs, or else refuse to sit on them, and they will become chilled. Many estates keep their eggs in incubators until the first chips show, and then transfer them to the nests in the coops.

The chicks need no food for the first twenty-four hours, and the pen must not be moved for the first few days after they have hatched. This is the most critical time of all. A hundred and one things can go wrong. Sometimes a hen will kill her chicks after dark, and a theory here is that she mistakes them for mice. Mostly, though, this happens when day-old chicks have been introduced to a hen that has been sitting out her time on "crock eggs".

Nowadays dry-feeding is favoured in preference to boiled mash. It is wasteful, though, because a lot of the crumbs become scattered and lost in the grass, and in wet weather any exposed food becomes mushy and unfit for consumption. The broody hen is best fed on boiled wheat for the first few weeks. Hard corn is harmful to young chicks, and they will most certainly eat this if it is available. A supply of grit is essential, and they must have access to fresh water at all times. Water-fountains can be obtained from any shop selling poultry appliances, and these ensure a regular supply of *shallow* water. Chicks are not only easily drowned, but a soaking will be followed by a fatal chill within a few hours.

There is one aspect of pheasant-rearing which the keeper, whether amateur or professional, is unable to control . . . *the weather!* A heavy thunderstorm, lasting perhaps less than an hour, will drown any chicks caught out in it, and those which manage to get back to the protection of their mother will probably die of pneumonia. In spite of all the progress we have made, we are helpless when Nature herself decrees that we are not to be blessed with a good season.

Now let us take a look at the dedicated amateur rearer on the smallest possible scale. His efforts will be no less ardent than that of the professional keeper, his successes smaller, but his losses, proportionally, will be far greater.

REARING ON A VERY SMALL SCALE

Pheasant rearing for the amateur keeper presents just as many problems as it does for the full-time professional, the only difference being that the latter's livelihood depends upon his success, whilst the former has only the prospect of the coming season's sport at stake. It is a nerve-racking time for both, and I know from my own experience that I am heartily glad when the end of August comes round, and the survivors of my weeks of labour are finally committed to the uncertainties of life in the wild.

I rear all my pheasants on the lawn at home, and have the operation cut down to a fine art, mainly due to lack of space. I use only one pen, accommodating approximately twenty six-week-old poults, and have it so worked out that their enclosure is moved approximately three times per week, necessitating eighteen moves throughout the time in which they are under my control. This covers the complete length of one side of the lawn, leaving absolutely no room to spare. Having reached the end of my first session of rearing by approximately the first week in July, I then transfer the pen to the opposite side of the lawn where I embark upon the second phase of my programme, which is concluded about mid-August.

Now the professional gamekeeper has not this problem of space to contend with. He can move his pen daily, and his growing poults have double the amount of fresh grass to peck at. The two situations, although working towards the same end, namely providing a stock of pheasants with which to supplement the wild stock on the shoot, are completely different. The death of one chick to me represents a loss of perhaps fifty to my professional counterpart, so greater care must be given to each individual bird by myself.

DAY-OLD CHICKS IN PREFERENCE TO EGGS

Nowadays, I always buy day-old chicks in preference to a clutch of eggs. In the long run it is much more economical. A broody may sit twenty eggs, and perhaps hatch an average of say fifteen. Allowing for casualties of hatching, I could be left with as few as ten. I then have the same amount of work to do to rear these as I would have for my twenty day-old chicks. Therefore, over the last five years, I have resorted to buying these direct from a reputable game farm, and it has paid dividends.

EXPERIMENTING WITH AN INCUBATOR

I well remember some of my early experiments with hatching pheasant eggs. Initially, I bought an oil-heated incubator, fully convinced that this would save me the trouble of feeding and tending a broody-hen daily. For three whole weeks I religiously turned and sprinkled my eggs, refilled my oil lamp, trimmed the wick, kept a constant check on the temperature (the most difficult task of all!) and generally tried to adhere to every instruction in the booklet which had been supplied with the incubator. Consequently, I was bitterly disappointed when only seven eggs began chipping, and eventually three of these produced live healthy chicks, the remaining four failing to peck their way successfully through the shells. However, I determined to rear my

Pheasant chicks hatching out in an incubator   Photo: Guy Smith

127

three at any cost, but my luck was not due to change. The family, thrilled at seeing these little balls of fluff tottering about the sandy egg-tray, decided to take a photograph of them. I reluctantly agreed, regretting my decision a few minutes later when the healthiest of the three, a pure melanistic mutant, jumped in the air in alarm at the sudden flash of the camera, fell down the funnel of the heater, and probably holds the record for the youngest ever roast pheasant! I persevered with the remaining two, and then disaster struck again. As they grew stronger and more venturesome, they began perching on the heater itself, huddling against the gauze guard at night for warmth. I presume that one must have fluttered, and caused a draught, the flame setting fire to the other. Next morning, I saw yet another charred chick, his brother also having died, due to a combination of poisonous oil-fumes from the smouldering wick, and a night spent in the cold. That concluded my experiments with incubators, apart from using them as sick-quarters for those chicks who were suffering with some ailment or other and would surely perish if left with the rest of the brood, under the hen.*

REARING PHEASANTS UNDER AN INFRA-RED LAMP

The infra-red lamp has, in many cases today, replaced the broody hen. An alternative is the gas heater. Yet some experience and knowledge is necessary before purchasing this equipment if losses in both chicks and poults are to be avoided.

Whether operated by gas or electricity, a constant temperature is essential or the pheasant chicks will die either from cold or excess heat. Where calor gas is used, a regulator must be attached to the bottle so the temperature can be kept constant.

The average size brooder house to hold 100 chicks should be approximately 6 foot square (1.83 m), with a sloping roof, 5 foot (1.52 m) high at one end and 4 foot (1.22 m) at the other. **It must be weatherproof,** allowing ventilation and light from mesh-covered apertures protected by flaps. A 400-watt heater will give the right amount of light for the chicks. Some keepers prefer a red lamp which does not excite the chicks to the same extent as a white lamp, thus reducing feather pecking.

The chicks should be put under the lamp 24 hours after hatching out in the incubator, but in the early days a barrier will be necessary in order to keep them under the heat. This can be made from hardboard,

Editorial note: The small electric incubators now on the market can be very efficient, but they still require considerable care and attention.

or even strong cardboard, and should be circular so that they are prevented from crowding into a corner.

The brooder house must be warm when the chicks are put into it. A temperature of 32—35°C. is ideal.

If the chicks are seen to be huddling together then they are cold, but if they spread out to the furthermost points of the partition then they are too hot. They must be watched carefully. Generally they are hardy for the first twenty–four hours, during which time they require no food, but after that problems are likely to arise. They must always be watched, and attention must be paid to the outside temperature which can influence that of the interior. Hot sun beating down on the brooder house will send the thermometer soaring; a cloudy cool day will cause it to fall.

The lamp itself should be about 15 inches (38 cm) above the chicks during the first few days. A short run-out into the open can be made available after the first few days, weather permitting. See that food and water is available both inside and outside the house. If the weather is cold then no harm will be done by keeping the chicks indoors. Most early losses are caused by them becoming chilled.

After a couple of weeks or so the lamp can be raised a few inches. Ensure that the house is warm at night, and the chicks should be settled beneath the lamp before the temperature drops in the evening. Do not let them out into the run too early in the morning. Allow the day to warm up a little first.

As the chicks grow into poults they will become hardier, but the night temperature can fall considerably, even in summer, and so they must be shut in the house each night until they are about a month old. After the fifth week provided the heat is reduced gradually it can be turned off altogether.

The birds are growing fast now and need more space, so any remaining partitions should be removed. In warm weather they can be allowed to roost outside the house in the run, but it is a good idea to erect a few perches. Get them into the habit of going up to roost, because if they form the habit of sitting on the ground, once they are released into the open they will become easy prey for foxes.

The main food in the early stages should be game rearing crumbs or Turkey Starter crumbs. However pheasants are very fond of ants' eggs and aphids. If you can spare the odd broad bean branch from the vegetable garden, covered with black fly, your birds will appreciate it.

STRANGE EXPERIENCE

I had a strange experience one summer, during my rearing programme, which may be of help to others confronted with a similar situation, and could very well save them a few birds. One morning, about a week after I had started on the second stage of my trials and tribulations, I discovered that four chicks had wandered away from the hen during the night, and lay limp and lifeless in the run-out, obviously victims of the cold atmosphere. Somewhat disappointed, I placed the four of them on the rockery whilst I tended to the others, and then completely forgot about them! The sun rose high in the sky, and a scorching hot day began. Some hours later, on returning to look at my pheasants in the pen again. I heard a ''cheep-cheep'' from amongst the aubretia on the rockery, and, on further investigation, I saw my four ''dead'' week-old chicks hopping about in a lively fashion. I put them back amongst the rest of the brood, and it was impossible to tell which ones they were on the following morning! I lost no more that year. It is always worth putting a ''dead'' chick in the warmth for a few hours on the off-chance of a revival, whether it be in warm sunshine, or in a cardboard box in front of the fire.

THE PROBLEMS OF RELEASE-PENS

It is a relief to both professional and amateur keepers when the month of August arrives, and the time comes to take those hand-reared pheasants, which have been nursed throughout the summer, to the woods. On estates where large numbers of birds are reared, the earlier hatches will already be in the woodlands, but, for most, August is the long awaited month. The trials and tribulations of the earlier stages of the rearing programme are now past, and the novice may well think that his worries are over. Certainly the ''teething'' troubles are gone, and periods when one anxiously watches day-old chicks with bated breath, wondering if they are going to survive, but the most vital obstacle of all lies ahead now, the introduction of the birds into the wide, wide world.

Release-pens are vital to the success of those keepers, and amateurs as well, who rear their birds in any quantity. Indeed, even the man who relies on a mere handful of poults to supplement his wild stock, will benefit from some sort of vermin proof enclosure in which to turn them, whilst they acclimatise themselves to the outside world. However, there are some instances where a release pen is an impracticable proposition, and then one is faced with the problem of combating the enemies of game without the satisfaction of knowing that at least one's birds are reasonably secure for the first week or two.

RELEASE PENS MUST BE SECURE

A release pen which allows vermin access, because of rusted wire-netting, neglect, or poor construction, is worse than having no pen at all. It is virtually a death-trap for the pheasant poults, and the following account serves to illustrate the importance of a *secure* enclosure.

A few years ago I experienced, at first hand, one of the major problems which besets the professional gamekeeper; namely the responsibility of looking after a large release-pen with several hundred eight-week old poults in it. As it happened, I was paying a social visit to a retired gamekeeper friend, when one of the young neighbouring keepers arrived.

It transpired that when he had gone to feed his birds in the 'big pen', he discovered that there was a terrier in there as well. He had noticed this particular dog in the vicinity several times before, and now his suspicions were proved correct. Somehow, it had obtained entry. He went into the enclosure after it, but it soon eluded him in the three acres or so of dense undergrowth inside the wire-netting. Now, he sought help in locating it before it was able to carry out any extensive damage.

The three of us returned to the scene of the trouble. My two companions carried their guns, whilst I was handed a length of rope, in the hope that the intruder might be taken alive. I was supposed to try and lassoo it, for I had no intention of grabbing hold of a semi-wild dog with my bare hands. Failing that, there would be no alternative other than to shoot it, for it could not be left to roam amongst the poults overnight whilst its owner was sought.

The first thing I noticed, as we opened the gate, and stepped inside, was the utter stillness. Poults perched precariously on low bushes everywhere, which made not the slight attempt to flutter away at our approach. Altogether, the setting was too peaceful for there to be an enemy abroad.

I took up my stance at one corner, whilst the other two separated, and walked around the perimeter, until they met halfway. None of us either saw or heard anything which signified the presence of a dog. It was obvious that he had gone, and it was probable that he would return when we had left. A check was made of the wire-netting, and also the series of small funnels by which the poults would eventually make their entry into the outside world. Everywhere was found to be firm, with no sign of an entry having been forced. How, then, had the dog got in? The wire was certainly much too high for the most agile terrier to jump over. Obviously, it had escaped by the same route as it had come in, whatever that was.

131

·Pheasants penned, in open-release, for laying, at the ratio of six hens to one cock. Note the provision of a water fountain, in the foreground, which must be kept filled.

Coops housed in a wire run, to protect pheasant chicks from vermin, when reared in the open-release system.

Prevention cannot be effectively executed if the malady remains undiagnosed, so my keeper friend was faced with no alternative but to spend many hours, which he could ill afford to spare, in constant vigil.

Release-pens are always a worry, no matter how secure they appear. The fact that the keeper has a large proportion of his birds concentrated in a very small area, increases the chance of a major disaster. This same friend of mine, only a week or so before the incident which I have related, lost a hundred poults in a torrential thunderstorm. Totally unavoidable, but, nevertheless, heartbreaking.

Very few of these enclosures have an overhead covering. The majority of them incorporate a small spinney, or a section of a large wood. Trees are a necessity if the birds are to learn to go up to roost, so any form of roofing is out of the question. Therefore, the main threat comes from the sky; from winged vermin which seize the opportunity of an easy meal. Let us take a brief look at the species of vermin which constitute the greatest danger to our young poults in these pens.

Assuming that the wire is strong, and there are no gaps, foxes should not be able to gain entry, although my recent experience with the terrier leads me to believe that nothing is impossible. With small mesh, stoats and weasels should be kept at bay, although the grey squirrel will find no difficulty in dropping down from the branches above. However, he is interested purely in the grain which is lying on the ground, so is more of a nuisance than a menace. Rats will find their way in almost anywhere, so tunnels of bait should be situated at strategic points on the outside of the pen, together with a network of humane traps.

Regarding winged vermin, the corvine tribe are usually only a danger at hatching time, when they will search out the most carefully hidden nest, and devour eggs or very young chicks. Hawks are apt to become interested in a confined bunch of accessible pheasant poults, the worst offender of which is, undoubtedly, the sparrow-hawk. However, these birds of prey are not to be found in sufficient numbers to kill more than the odd bird. Likewise, the occasional rogue buzzard may choose to remain motionless in a tree overlooking the release-pen, and keep his larder well supplied by dropping down, from time to time, on any unsuspecting bird which wanders beneath him.

There is no doubt that the worst threat of all comes from domestic pets, cats and dogs. A cat is capable of climbing almost anything, and I have seen for myself what a determined dog can accomplish.

A release-pen is always a calculated risk. In an attempt to protect the poults from the dangers of the wide world, they are being confined to a place where, should danger strike, then the losses will be heavy. It is a price which we have to pay for combining artificiality with Nature.

OPEN RELEASE

I have given much thought to the problem of releasing my birds, and have experimented to no small degree. Three-quarters of my shoot consists of Forestry Commission plantations, and to turn my poults straight into these would be to present the vermin with an easy and appetising series of meals for the first few days following release, Therefore, my birds must be turned out on to the surrounding farmland, using the most suitable cover avialable.

In my early days on this particular shoot, I hit upon the idea of turning the broody hen loose with the pheasants in order that they would benefit from her presence in the initial period. When a late harvest was apparent, I released them into a field of barley, knowing that they had a full fortnight at least before any attempt was made to harvest this crop, and by that time they would be old enough to look after themselves. It was a success the first time that I tried it, but I met with disaster the following year, simply by sheer bad luck. It happened that the farmer had discarded an old corrugated iron poultry "arc" in some undergrowth bordering his barley field. I never gave it a second glance, but the broody hen must have recognised it as a prospective home for herself and her poults, possibly having lived in one in her earlier farmyard days. As a result she took her family there on their first night out in the open, and Reynard must have had a very pleasant surprise when he came upon them there during his nocturnal prowlings. It was a bitter disappointment to me when I discovered the remains of his carnage, but it only made me more determined to find other ways of outwitting him the following year.

I still persisted with the idea of taking the mother hen to the shoot, along with the poults, but experience had taught me the dangers involved in doing this, so I decided upon a slightly different mode of release the next August. One of the farms incorporated in my shooting rights, borders the large area of Forestry plantations, and is situated in a small hollow just below the main woodlands. The farmer allows his poultry to range freely outside his back door, and sometimes has to remove one or two of the more venturesome hens from the kitchen! My plan now was to release my pheasants directly outside the farmhouse, within a distance of some ten yards from the back door. His adjacent orchard, with its long grass, would provide all the cover they needed, and when the birds felt inclined to wander, they would automatically make their way towards my woods.

I put my plan into action, and all went smoothly with the exception of one young cock pheasant which decided to test his newly found power of flight. The moment that he was out of the large wicker basket he struck upwards, towards the house, and flew into the bathroom window with a resounding bump! However, the pane of glass withstood the impact, and for the next half hour the dazed bird tottered, somewhat uncertainly, up and down the roof of the porch below, until he finally plucked up sufficient courage to flutter down to join his colleagues in the orchard below. All seemed very much at home, including the hen.

However, the success of my scheme was not fully realised until the following evening when the farmer went out after dark to shut up his roosting poultry in the hen-house. He thought that the small shed seemed rather crowded, and returned to the house in order to fetch his torch, so that he might see the reason for the apparent jostling for perching places amongst his fowls. Imagine his surprise when he saw, by the light of his old bicycle-lamp, my broody hen, and a dozen or so of the pheasants, all prepared to spend the night in the comfort of this wooden building, and some of his regular layers being forced to squat on the floor as a result! This state of affairs continued for the next few days, the number of pheasants decreasing slowly each night until finally they all took to the wild.

I am convinced that, under the circumstances, this latter method of release of mine is the best so far. In this way not only do I avoid submitting the hen to the dangers of prowling vermin, but I ensure that once her job of looking after my pheasants has finished, she will happily join up with the farmer's poultry, and perhaps be suitable for use again next year if I require her services.

Life is very difficult for the man who is unable to operate a release-pen. He is deprived of the main essential in introducing his poults into their natural wild state, and he has to make the most of local conditions to ensure that they are given the best possible start to their new life.

PHEASANTS ON SHOOTING DAYS

The pheasant can be one of the most difficult shots in the field, or it can be one of the easiest, depending on how it is presented.

Hand-reared birds are naturally apt to be tamer than their counterparts hatched in the wild. They have been brought up to accept

Ring-necked Pheasant

Man, to rely upon him for food daily, answering the keeper's whistle night and morning. Consequently, they are hardly likely to be afraid of him until they have learned what shooting is all about, and by that time they will have offered themselves as simple targets.

One of the most important aspects in presenting worthwhile pheasants is the type of terrain over which you shoot. if the ground is flat, then it will be more difficult. A pheasant always prefers to run when danger threatens, and only flies as a last resort. Thus you have got to make your birds take to the wing at each drive.

A good method is to stretch a role of wire–netting across the end of the covert between the guns and the advancing birds. The mesh should be small, so that the pheasants do not squeeze through and continue running. This will certainly make them take to the wing, and if the fence is 75–100 yards (68–91 m approx) away from the guns, then by the time the birds reach them they should have gained a respectable height.

In upland territory it is much easier to shoot high pheasants – provided that you drive them from high to low ground. An ideal site is two wooded hillsides with a valley between them. If the pheasants can be persuaded to cross from one to the other, then the guns standing below will have some first class shooting.

Where possible, feeding points should be situated on high ground. In this way birds will be in the right place at the beginning of a day's shooting.

Of course, with walking–up pheasants the same quality of shooting cannot be expected, but here the mode of sport is different. The actual shot is only part of the enjoyment. The reader will enjoy working his dog, trying to find that elusive cock that evaded him the week before, and when the bird finally breaks from cover it will probably be just when you least expect it. You may be standing awkwardly on a steep slope as your dog flushes the bird behind you, and it is difficult to turn and shoot. Or there will be a thick bush between you and the pheasant.

One cannot compare driving and walking–up. They both have their merits. The latter, once used extensively on all the big estates, is now generally regarded as the sport of the rough shooter.

REDUCING SURPLUS COCK PHEASANTS AT THE CLOSE OF THE SEASON

As most sportsmen are aware, there are times when there is an abundance of cock pheasants remaining at the end of the season. These can be as detrimental to game prospects as the vermin which we are constantly waging war upon. The cockpheasant is an aggressive bird and seldom will he tolerate a rival on his own territory. Most of us, from time to time, have witnessed a duel of vicious claws between two of these birds in the spring, and if a number were fighting at nesting time it could result in unsettled hens and late nesting. Therefore, the cocks must be thinned out as the season draws to a close.

The usual method is to organise a series of 'cocks only' days, and generally this suffices. However, this necessary operation can be thwarted during the second half of January by heavy snowfalls during which it is impossible to shoot at all. Hence, we have too many male birds remaining amongst our existing stock, and something must be done about it.

After February 1st it is too late to shoot game legally, so the task falls on either the gamekeeper or the shooting tenant.

The best place for a single gun to make a bag of cock pheasants is at the feeding points, but this must be done with as little disturbance as possible, for otherwise all of one's hand-reared birds will be dispersed, probably over the boundaries where they may well fall prey to an unscrupulous neighbour. Thus, the rifle must play its part, once again.

Let us assume that there are three main feeding points in the woodlands on your shoot. A few days after an organised shoot the birds will be back here feeding in numbers, answering your whistle and scratching for grain within a few feet of where you are standing. The cocks, with their splendid winter plumage at its best, present an ideal target for the shooter.

Feeding should, whenever possible, be carried out at the same time each day. Consequently, the pheasants will be awaiting your arrival at about eight o'clock in the morning and four o'clock in the afternoon. It is best to choose the latter time for thinning out cocks. An early morning onslaught may cause the majority to desert your land in search of safer pastures, and they will have all day in which to do it, whereas with the coming of dusk they will be disinclined to wander in search of another roost.

Arrive at your destination a good hour before the normal time, and do not whistle the birds to feed. Some of the greedier ones will already be anticipating your coming, and as you approach the clearing take the first one you see. Then, station yourself in a good vantage position from which you will be able to ambush the early arrivals as they wander in. Once the main lot begin arriving stop shooting and commence feeding as normal. Shot birds must be retrieved at once.

This process will take a week, perhaps longer, and if you are averaging three kills each afternoon then you are doing well. Do not forget that Sunday shooting of game is illegal, and you could find yourself in trouble with the law if you ignore this. The Sabbath will provide a welcome lull for any birds which have become suspicious, and by Monday their confidence will have been restored. You can also rotate this form of shooting around your feeding points, and when the season finally draws to a close, your stock of birds will have benefited as well as being undisturbed.

WHICH SPECIES TO REAR

Very few amateurs spare much thought to the species of pheasants which they rear. An order for pheasants eggs usually results in a mixture of Old English or Ring-Necks unless specified. However, it is as well to consider details. You have a lot of work in front of you the day those eggs arrive, and if the job is worth doing at all, it is worth doing properly.

The Melanistic has the least inclination of all pheasants to wander. I found, though, when I attempted to introduce them on to my own shoot, that they were turning up on farms lower down in the valley, so I can only conclude that they are not keen on high ground. My Ring-Necks remained more or less in the vicinity so I chose to continue with this variety.

It is a good idea, wherever your shoot is situated, and whatever species comprises the bulk of your stock, to include one or two Chinese pheasants each season. They show up easily with their light coloured plumage, and one can thus determine, more or less, the movements of one's birds.

My favourite, though, is the Old English with his splendid colourings, strutting through the woodlands, a king in his own domain. He is the wiliest of all, a true reward for months of toil and anxiety during the rearing season.

Pheasant rearing is probably one of the most frustrating aspects of a shooting man's career, but success can be rewarding enough to make all the difficulties worthwhile. One never stops learning, but there is great satisfaction to be gained from the knowledge that one is playing one's part in helping to increase a dwindling wild pheasant population throughout the country.

CHAPTER 16

Stocking with Partridge

THE DECLINE AND RISE OF THE PARTRIDGE

At long last the partridge is re-establishing itself. After a decline which almost threatened extinction, the most loved of all our game birds is gradually making a noticeable return to the rural scene. However, it is mostly the *Frenchman* (the red-legged partridge) which we see today rather than its cousin, the grey English bird which at one time dominated the species in this country.

Lincolnshire and Norfolk are possibly the most ideally suited counties in the whole of the British Isles as far as the partridge is concerned. There are a variety of reasons for this, the most important one being the intensity of agriculture. This bird is more at home in fields of potatoes, clover, and market garden produce, than in more natural surroundings. It will nest in the most ridiculous places imaginable, and there are many reports of a clutch of eggs being hatched and reared within a yard of a main railway line, and once a hen bird chose an open 'cold-frame' on a small-holding!

The main cause of the decline of the partridge was the widespread use of toxic sprays on growing crops, and **not** over-shooting, as was once commonly supposed. It is a good thing for coveys to be shot hard, for an over-populated area of these birds can only lead to outbreaks of disease. A happy medium must be the aim at all times. However, with the restrictions imposed on these poisonous sprays, the coveys gradually began increasing, helped, of course, by gamekeepers who supplemented the stock on their ground by hand-rearing a few birds each year, along with their pheasants. For a few seasons partridge shooting was almost non-existent, each landowner and shooting tenant fearing lest he wiped out his few surviving birds.

In recent years some good bags of partridges have been recorded on the eastern counties estates during the early part of the season. Lincolnshire is possibly more suited to partridge driving than anywhere else, for the flat countryside enables a gamekeeper to watch the flight of the birds when sprung, and determine the fields and flight–line which they take.

It is a great pity for the partridge that the combine–harvester has now almost totally replaced the old-fashioned binder, for no longer do we find those fields of tall stubble which were so loved by these birds in days gone by, providing them with both gleanings and cover. Added to this, the burning of stubble after the harvest only serves to drive the coveys elsewhere, and it is not until the fire scarred fields have come under the plough that they will return.

Most of us are familiar with the grating call of the partridge in the morning and evening, appearing to come from a ploughed field; but although we may stand and watch for lengthy periods, it is often very hard to spot the birds until they suddenly run, in swift darting movements, across the furrows. They only take to the wing as a last resort, usually when danger threatens.

The absence of foxes in Lincolnshire is favourable to the partridge, for this bird, which never roosts in trees as does the pheasant, is easy meat for Reynard as he prowls in search of prey after dark. Therefore, the coveys in this county are spared one factor so detrimental to their survival. The abundance of potato fields is a haven for them, and until the end of September they are assured of ample cover. Then they must turn to the sugar–beet and cabbage fields.

The weather is largely responsible for the size of the partridge population, and therefore the drier climate of East Anglia is acceptable to these birds. Long wet periods at hatching time, along with heavy thunderstorms, can virtually wipe out all the chicks. The sight of a pair of adult birds together, during the summer months, is usually a sure sign that they have lost their brood. However, if one sees a single parent bird, it is a fair assumption that it is the cock, and that the hen is sitting somewhere in the vicinity. On the other hand, we may be confronted, during a country ramble, by a partridge dragging a 'broken wing', allowing us to advance so far towards it before it flutters away again. This is the hen bird, attempting to decoy us away from her nearby nest, using the oldest ruse known to the partridge.

BREEDING PROBLEMS IN THE WILD

The hen partridge takes great trouble in selecting her nesting site during the spring, and then, incredibly, may finally decide on some precarious place where the danger from vermin and trespassers is doubled! During the pre–war era when almost every field held its own covey of partridges, the gamekeepers used to practise what was known as the Euston System to combat the perils of badly situated nests (see below). Although this system was fraught with danger, it did reduce the period in which the eggs were exposed to danger.

The favourite food of partridge in the wild is ants' eggs, but there are not sufficient of these to constitute a staple diet. Modern agricultural methods in the form of ploughing-in the stubble soon after the harvest has also deprived this bird of much natural food. Contrary to popular belief, the coveys flushed from stubble-fields are not there solely in search of fallen grain, but rather the weeds which grow there. Today they are even denied these.

Regrettably our native bird, the 'grey' or 'English' partridge, has largely been replaced by the red-legged French one. The latter is hardly comparable to the former where parenthood is concerned. It never covers the eggs when leaving the nest, and sometimes follows the example of the cuckoo in that it lays its eggs in the grey bird's nest, and leaves her to do the rest of the work! This French bird sometimes deserts its own nest after the first week or so, and in many ways contributes to its own downfall. The two species rarely mix, and with a greater abundance of the redlegs, the hope that one day these delightful English birds will again reach their former numbers seems somewhat remote.

The partridge usually begins laying about the middle of April, depending on the weather, of course. She lays four or five eggs a week until eventually she has a clutch of between twelve and eighteen. The real dangers begin, though, as soon as the chicks begin to hatch. The chick has a special 'egg tooth' which drops off after a few days outside the shell. For the first twenty-four hours it needs no food, and at this stage the weather can either make or break the future partridge population. A heavy thunderstorm results in the majority of the birds either being drowned or else contracting pneumonia through becoming chilled. Late frosts can be equally detrimental, and long periods of wet weather can induce *gapes*, little worms which grow in the birds windpipes, and eventually choke them. Coccidiosis is another disease brought on by cold and wet, affecting the stomach and liver, and causing the victims to waste away. However, both these diseases are more prevalent in birds reared in captivity than those in the wild.

Drought, however, troubles the partridge little, and it seems to obtain all the moisture it needs from the morning dews. Consequently, the summer of 1976 was the tonic needed by the ailing partridge population. Another such season would considerably help it on its way to recovery. The future of this grand little bird rests with the elements, and in spite of all the efforts of conservationists, this is the key to its future survival.

TEST OF MARKSMANSHIP

The partridge is the real favourite with most shooting men. It is a bird which tests the finest of marksmen, and is an integral part of the rural scene. A few years ago, it was feared that this little game-bird might become extinct. Its dwindling numbers were blamed on over-shooting, yet this was not the case. Toxic-sprays on farm crops were largely responsible for this alarming situation, but, at last, a major withdrawal of these has seen a marked rise in the partridge population. Indeed, in many parts of the British Isles this bird is re-asserting itself, and game-preservers are pleased to see sizeable coveys, where previously they had seen only barren birds.

The weather, too, is an important factor governing the rise or decline of the partridge, so susceptible is it to climatic conditions. Deluges during the crucial hatching period can reduce the number of birds throughout the country by almost half, and ruthless sportsmen, who pursue the remaining adult birds throughout the following shooting season with the same eagerness which they would show towards an abundance of coveys, are pushing the partridge beyond its limits.

SUITABILITY FOR PARTRIDGES

However, if your shoot is suitable for partridge, yet the existing wild stocks are low, you can do no better than to hand-rear a few, in the same way that you have attempted to increase your pheasants. You must have the right kind of terrain, though, or else you are just wasting your time, and within a week of the release date there will not be a partridge to be seen on the place. Root crops and/or clover are an essential, for your birds will not remain in grass fields alone. Modern harvesting methods do not allow for the long stubble, so loved by the partridge in years gone by, when there was ample gleanings from the stocked wheat.

Partridges are no more difficult to rear, although the eggs and day-old chicks are about three times as expensive, than pheasants. Of course, if you can catch up a few stock birds in the early spring, and take your own eggs, the whole project will be very much cheaper. However, to begin with, an all-out assault on vermin is essential, otherwise you will merely be providing the various species of predators with some very easy meals! Traps and gun must work overtime during February and March, and you must not overlook one of the deadliest enemies of the partridge—*the hedgehog.* If these seemingly harmless creatures are allowed to breed prolifically, then your few wild birds will not stand an earthly of rearing a brood, for Mr. Prickly is the keenest of all egg-hunters, rivalling even the carrion crow in his diligent searching, for he can forage amongst the hedgerows and undergrowth where the partridge has made her nest.

THE EUSTON SYSTEM

There are two ways in which one can attempt to rear a few partridges for the small shoot. I think a brief mention of the famous *Euston System* is worthwhile, although you need a combination of experience and luck to attain real success. The partridge is only rivalled by the mallard in its stupidity of choice of nesting sites. It has been known to lay within a few feet of main roads and railway lines, seemingly oblivious of the nearby activity. Likewise, a bird which nests in the open is virtually inviting the corvine tribe to help themselves, and this is where the Euston System comes to the rescue.

First, you must locate your nests, and prepare the appropriate number of broody bantams (preferred to hens where partridges are concerned), and see that you have an ample supply of dummy eggs. Armed with the latter, you must disturb the sitting bird, and, whilst she is away, exchange her eggs for yours. Thus, a short time later, your broodies will be continuing the incubation of the partridge eggs, whilst these game birds are happily sitting out their time on the crock ones. Then, as soon as the eggs are ready to hatch, you must go and disturb the sitting partridge once more, and swop the eggs again in her absence. Thus, if all goes well, she will rear her own chicks, the real eggs having been guarded by you during the vital period of incubation. The thieving crows, if they have located the nest, will have done no harm. Of course, Reynard might well have found the sitting partridge, in which case your bantam will have to complete the job of hatching. Bantams are good mothers, anyway, so you have an equal chance of success. I tried this system once on a small shoot which I had at the time, and was successful with two nests out of three. It is time-saving, too, for you have not got the job of rearing the chicks, and releasing them.

PARTRIDGE REARING ON A LARGER SCALE

If you are considering rearing partridges in any number, then your shoot must have an abundance of arable land. Woodlands and grazing land will not hold partridges, and unless you have the right cover available then you are wasting your time. A good relationship with the farm-workers is essential, because their co-operation, particularly during mowing time, can save many birds which have nested in the long grass. You must try to protect your wild stock whilst at the same time attempting to rear birds to supplement it.

We have already discussed the Euston System and, for argument's sake, abandoned it. The pens and coops are ready, and having already acquired the necessary number of broody bantams we are ready to begin. Coops must be sited at least thirty yards apart, and not beneath hedges or trees where the sun will be kept off the growing chicks. The first eggs will be ready from mid-April onwards, and the hen partridge lays approximately four or five each week until her clutch of anything between 12 and 18 is complete. As in the case of pheasants it is desirable, where possible, to put the eggs under the bantams only when they begin to chip. The partridge chick has a special egg-tooth which drops off only a few hours after emerging from the shell, and then it needs no food for the first twenty-four hours. Modern crumbs and pellet-food will provide it with all the nourishment it requires, but if ants' eggs are obtainable these will be an added aid to the growth of the bird. I must stress, though, that earth-ants are preferable to wood-ants. For the first week feed every 2–3 hours, moving the pens daily as the birds grow, until at six weeks you are moving them at least twice each day. There is an awful lot of work to partridge rearing, and the weather will either be your friend or your enemy.

The birds should be moved to their permanent quarters at six weeks, the foster-mothers remaining in the coops so that the poults can return to their protection each night until the time comes when they prefer to 'juk' on their own. Now remove the bantams but leave the empty coops. The birds still associate them with their upbringing, and this helps to hold them in the vicinity. Root crops are essential for holding your partridges at this stage.

ENGLISH OR FRENCH?

Regrettably the French partridge (Redleg) is nowadays much more prolific than the Grey or English Partridge. The two species do not mix, although sometimes the redleg adopts the habits of the cuckoo, and lays in the grey bird's nest, leaving her with the task of bringing up the chicks. If you happen to come across a nest containing eggs during April, the identity of the bird which

French Partridge

attempts to decoy you with the broken-wing ruse is no indication which species the eggs have been laid by. A quick look will tell you all you want to know. If the eggs are brown or olive grey they have been laid by the English bird, but if they are buff with red spots or purple blotches they belong to the redleg. The latter's eggs hatch out a day earlier than those of her courterpart.

WINTER FEEDING

Once your partridges have established themselves in the wild, your duties have not ended. With modern farming methods the stubble is not left for lengthy periods after the harvest, but often ploughed in within'a matter of a week or so. This stubble contains a variety of weeds which are essential food for the partridge, and it must be replaced by hand-feeding. Likewise, in times of hard weather unless you feed your coveys they will either die of starvation or else stray on to a neighbouring shoot. A mixture of wheat and barley is ideal, and should be fed in remaining root fields, and along sheltered banks and hedgerows. One must be vigilant with regard to poachers, though, for should these feeding places become known amongst the poaching fraternity, they have only to lie in wait, and will account for the bulk of a covey with a couple of barrels.

Drought has little affect on partridges, and the birds seem to be capable of obtaining all the moisture they require from the morning dews. The food of the adult partridge in the wild is estimated to be 50 per cent insects and 50 per cent vegetable. However, their position today is so precarious that it is the game-preserver who determines their future. It is up to the amateur keeper to play his part, even if he only hatches one sitting of eggs each season.

REARING PARTRIDGES ON THE LAWN
Alternatively, you can rear your partridges, either from eggs or day-old chicks, under bantams on the lawn in more or less the same way that you reared your pheasants. The first fortnight is the most frustrating when the chicks do not appear to grow at all. Then, suddenly, their progress is visible, day by day. Commercial feeder-crumbs and growers'-pellets make the job much easier, a far cry from the days when it was necessary to boil eggs and mash. During the first few days the chicks should be fed every two hours, then, as they grow, regulated, until finally they are accustomed to being fed mornings and evenings only. The coops should be moved daily, and I would refer you to this procedure in the chapter on pheasants, thereby ensuring that you obtain the maximum number of moves on a small piece of ground without over-lapping.

RELEASING YOUR BIRDS INTO THE WILD
Eventually, the day of release arrives, and if your birds have been feather-pecking you will be heartily relieved. You must then determine whether or not to employ the services of a release-pen, depending of course, on your availability to supervise it.

You are now congratulating yourself on a successful rearing season as September 1st approaches, and there is evidence that your birds are still around. Now you must attempt to strike a happy medium between conservation and shooting, bearing in mind that next season's stock birds will depend on how well you manage the next five months. Of course, in root crops and clover, partridges can be walked-up comfortably during September and early October. They will invariably rise within range unless your dog is in the habit of foraging on, well ahead of the guns.

SHOOTING
There is one point worth mentioning here, and I can do no better than refer the reader to the advice given by Colonel Peter Hawker

in the last century, that "grand-daddy of all shooting men". Hawker *never* pursued partridges before about ten o'clock in the morning when the dew was off the root fields. This still applies today. Neither the partridge nor the pheasant is fond of wet roots, preferring the shelter of deeper undergrowth. Likewise, it is unfair to the coveys to pursue them right up until dusk. They will be tired, and having been pushed over the boundaries on to a neighbour's ground, they may decide to stay there on the morrow.

However, as October progresses, the partridges will become wilder. The young birds will have learnt what shooting is all about. The potato harvesters will have been at work, and the cover will be sparse. Now, your only means of obtaining a shot at the coveys will be by *driving* them to the guns. Unless you are in a syndicate which employs a few beaters on shooting days, you will have to devise a plan whereby half the guns stand behind a hedge whilst the remainder walk the field towards them. Naturally, great care must be taken, for wild shooting could result in injury or worse.

DRIVING

Even if there are only three or four guns, it is still possible to drive partridges, providing that you study the layout of the land beforehand. The birds will be pushed towards cover which is acceptable to them, far more easily than they will be driven on to barren fields. After your first few attempts, you will soon see which direction the coveys like to fly once they are sprung. I remember, one November afternoon, during my early shooting days, being out after partridge with an elderly farmer. There were just the two of us, and when we spied a small covey in the centre of a grass field, I abandoned any idea of getting within range of them. However, my companion stated that he would make a wide detour over the adjoining fields, which would bring him behind the opposite hedgerow, some three hundred yards away. I was to allow him a quarter of an hour, and then begin walking across the grass, diagonally, and not directly towards where he would be waiting. I gave him twenty minutes to be on the safe side, and then I climbed over the gate, and into the field. Hardly had I advanced a dozen yards before that covey whirred up, making for the exact spot where my companion had said they would. Two shots rang out, almost as one, and I saw two partridges drop, and then bounce on the grass. This was a perfect example, not only of a man who knew his partridges, but of one who knew his *ground*.

PAIRING UP

Partridges are usually pairing up towards the end of January, unless the weather happens to be particularly hard. Therefore, no sportsman worthy of the name will consider shooting them after Christmas. As far as pheasants are concerned, he can restrict himself to ''cocks only'', which actually benefits the stock, for an abundance of cocks is undesirable. However, the difficulty entailed in attempting to pick the cock partridges out of a covey, restricts their shooting altogether. It is a good thing, though, if we are to build up our partridges again.

My present shoot is virtually devoid of partridges, for these game birds favour lowlands rather than uplands. Yet, occasionally, I hear that magical sound of partridges, calling to each other, preparatory to jukking in the sheep fields for the night. Only last season I flushed a large covey of perhaps twenty birds, but I held my fire, for it was late in the season, and had they suddenly taken a liking to my land, then I had no wish to discourage them at the start.

One fears, and hopes, for the future of this, the grandest of all sporting birds, in this age of ''progress''. However, I believe that they *will*, given time, increase again to something like pre-war numbers. The shooting man is required to play a major role in this.

CHAPTER 17

Woodcock and Snipe

WOODCOCK

One of the most delightful little visitors to our rural scene during the winter months is the woodcock. His arrival, usually from the Scandinavian countries, is heralded by the November moon, and, sure enough, within 24 hours of its rising, this small bird with the long bill will be flushed from amongst piles of dead leaves, dying bracken and dense rhododendron bushes. The timing of this migration to winter quarters is one of the miracles of Nature. It is not just a matter of weeks, or even days, but of *hours!*

Although the woodcock is of the wader species, it does not frequent marshy areas and foreshores, as does its cousins the snipe and curlew. It prefers the dry shelter of woodlands where it can forage in the undergrowth after insects, undisturbed.

Woodcock

150

"Cock For'ard!"

The woodcock is, without a doubt, our most sought after game bird, prized by sportsmen far more than the conventional pheasant. It is the traditional will-o'-the-wisp of the woods, a silent flier whose zig-zag course puts even the most adept marksman to a severe test. During the course of a day's shooting, when pheasants are breaking from the coverts towards the waiting line of guns, the most stirring cry of all will be heard from one of the beaters, "cock up" or "cock for'ard". The true sportsman will feel the blood course through his veins at those very words. The novice will be inclined to panic, so keen is he to secure his first 'cock. Many of the older, experienced beaters fling themselves flat on their faces, giving this means of precaution as a reason for having attained their three score and ten! The sight of that small brown bird, swerving and weaving its way through the trees and bushes, is often too much for the beginner, and, forgetting all else, he will wildly let fly to the danger of everyone present.

The Bols Prize

Some years ago, Messrs. Bols of Holland offered a badge, and a bottle of their prized apricot brandy, to sportsmen anywhere in the world who achieved a "right and left" at woodcock, i.e. by killing

Four woodcock, but all shot singly. No Bols Prize this time!

Photo: Calvin Williams

two birds, consecutively, one with each barrel, without removing the gun from the shoulder between shots. Subsequent "rights and lefts" would earn the holder "bars" to his badge, accompanied by further bottles of liqueur. The only condition being that two witnesses testified to the feat. The number of men who have so far achieved this represents a small minority of the shooting men of the world, due, not only to the woodcock's erratic flight, which makes it a difficult, sometimes impossible, target, but to the fact that woodcock are seldom flushed in pairs. They are lone feeders. I remember one late autumn day, many years ago, when I was a guest at a shooting party at Norfolk. The keeper stated, before we set out, that the "cock should've come in on the November moon". How right he was! In a wood of some twenty acres or so, we flushed no fewer than 23 of these birds, *all singly*. Not once did we put up a pair of them together!

Resident Woodcock

Norfolk, of course, is ideally suited to accommodate those woodcock flying in across the North Sea who are looking for the first acceptable tract of countryside with ample woodlands. However, not all woodcock migrate. A very small percentage of them remain behind and breed. I saw an adult bird only this last summer, and I knew full well that this was the cock bird foraging for food, whilst the hen tended her chicks. More than likely, the young, if successfully reared, will choose to remain here. An age-old argument exists concerning the woodcock carrying her young, a myth which dates back to the beginning of time. Reports have been received of this strange means of transportation, but not once has sufficient proof been shown to substantiate it. I have certainly never witnessed it, so I am in no position either to confirm or deny it, but I feel that, was this a common occurrence amongst the woodcock population, then it would most certainly have been observed by reliable ornithologists.

Favourite Haunts

An aura of mystery has always surrounded the woodcock. Like the migratory duck and geese of the mudflats, there is always the question of whence they have come, and whither they will go when the spring comes round. Will they return next autumn? More than likely they will, for like many other species, they come back to the same place, often the same bush, year in year out. The woodcock's survival is in no danger, even at the expense of a bottle of apricot brandy and a marksman's badge, for its ability of self-preservation is second to none.

I have shot woodcock from the days of my boyhood. One usually knows the places in which to find them, the silver birch woods, or the thick rhododendron bushes. These are their favourite haunts, and I am always alert for them when I come across this type of terrain whilst out shooting.

However, over the past couple of seasons my methods of shooting 'cock have changed completely. Who hasn't, at some time or other, dreamt of that glorious right and left in front of two witnesses, the bottle of Bols' and the badge which accompanies it? It must be one of the most cherished prizes in the shooting field, but more important than that is the satisfaction which one will get from that glorious double shot. As a boy I remember my father almost achieving this feat. I was walking at his heels, one Saturday afternoon, labouring under the weight of three or four rabbits, when a woodcock rose from under some rhododendron bushes. He killed it cleanly, and had just removed the gun from his shoulder when another one rose. He mounted his gun again quickly, and killed this one as decisively as the first. However, the very fact that he had taken his gun down between shots meant that it did not constitute a ''right and left'', apart from the fact that he did not have the necessary witnesses present. That was the nearest which I have ever seen a sportsman come to achieving the honour.

Flighting Woodcock

To return to the woodcock on my own hill-shoot in Shropshire. I was waiting for duck with a friend by the small woodland pool one evening, just prior to Christmas, my ears tuned to pick up those magical wingbeats from overhead, when, without warning, something flitted silently over the treetops and across the water. It took some seconds for both of us to realise that it was a woodcock, and that period of hesitation cost us our bird. I did not note, at the time, the significance of this bird's presence at the pool prior to flighting time, merely passing it off as a chance encounter, for, as far as I knew, my large acreage of forestry plantation did not harbour a great number of woodcock.

Some weeks later, my friend and I were somewhat delayed in reaching this same pool for evening flight, having wasted the best part of an hour in searching for a winged cock pheasant, and as we approached the water two birds rose in the semi-gloom. My companion pulled off a right and left in fine style in the poor light. Remus, my yellow labrador, retrieved the first bird, a drake mallard, but when he returned with the second, I was astounded to find that it was no duck, but a *woodcock!* He had come so near to achieving the double, and it was ironical that the second bird had to be a duck.

From then onwards, woodcock became regular visitors to my flight-pond at deep dusk. The significance of their presence there still had not dawned on me, and I was under the impression that they were merely there in search of a drink.

Some weeks ago, I witnessed the largest number of woodcock which I have ever seen on my shoot. They appeared to have arrived under the November moon, for it was during the first duck-flight following this that we saw them. Dusk was turning to darkness, and I was on the verge of packing up, when the first bunch of 'cock arrived. They hurtled in low, well below the level of the surrounding fir trees, and our four barrels merely saluted them as they departed. Hastily, we reloaded, and had hardly done so before three more followed in the wake of the first. My companion was fortunate to drop one of these, and whilst I was busy directing the dog in the rushes, in an attempt to find it, some more arrived, and once again my partner scored a hit, the double still eluding him. We retrieved both birds, and decided that, as the light was now too poor for accurate shooting, it would be wiser to leave any more woodcock which might come in unmolested for another day.

Certainly, a right and left had been within our grasp that evening, from the fact that the birds had been there in numbers, not because the shooting was made any easier by flighting them in this way. Indeed, they present a far more difficult target when flighted. They put in an appearance, generally *after* the duck, when the light has almost gone, coming in low and fast, screened by the shadows of the surrounding trees. Unlike duck, when fired at, they do not rise in an attempt to gain maximum height as quickly as possible, but appear to fly even lower, swerving and jinking as they do so. They present a shot to tax the skill of the finest marksman, and he who manages a right and left in this way will have well and truly earned it.

Feeding Habits
However, I was not merely content to accept the fact that woodcock were visiting my flight-pond, from time to time, in numbers. I was curious to know the reason why, and it was some weeks before I eventually solved the mystery. I ruled out the possibility of there being food for them in the bed of the pool, for it has a hard shale bottom, being partly artificial, a natural spring having been diverted into a small, man-made reservoir. I examined

the surrounding banks. Grass had now grown over the earth which had been piled there after the excavations, but I could find nothing there which might have been of any interest to woodcock. Suddenly, the answer dawned on me. For weeks I had been dumping bags of small potatoes into the shallow end for the mallard and, on reflection, I noted that the birds had always been making for that part of the pool. The potatoes were the attraction, or rather the grubs and insects which the woodcock found in them.

Woodcock, like other birds, are apt to vary their feeding habits, according to the time of year, and the weather. Past records show that they only appear on my shoot during the early part of November, and then are absent until late January. I can only conclude that the advent of hard weather in the hills forces them to seek the comparative warmth and shelter of the valleys below. Whatever the reason, I am delighted that they find my humble woodland pool acceptable to them, from time to time.

SNIPE

Another bird, which is so similar, in many ways, to the woodcock, is the snipe. It, too, is mostly a winter visitor, although some pairs do remain behind to breed in this country.

The snipe, like the woodcock, is a severe test for any shooting man. Its erratic zig-zagging flight is hard to follow with one's gun, although I would regard it as slightly easier than the latter, simply

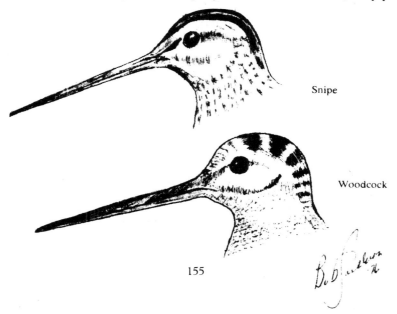

Snipe

Woodcock

155

because it is usually sprung in open marshland. The 'cock usually confuses the marksman by unerringly weaving its way between trees and rhododendrons, and often the undergrowth shields it from a charge of shot. There are two ways of successfully shooting snipe. One school believes in snapshooting the moment the bird rises, before it has a chance to begin its aerobatics, whilst the other prefers to wait until it has assumed a direct course of flight. The disadvantage of this latter method is that often the snipe has gained considerable distance, and although it may not actually be out of range, it will need a close pattern to account for a target so small. I, personally, prefer to fire at once.

Snipe nearly always favour marshland, although I have put them up out of root crops, far from the nearest water meadows. Usually, though, this has been during hard weather. Their main requirement is running water, and most streams will hold a few of these long-billed birds. Like duck, they feed throughout the night, and as dusk approaches, the wildfowler will hear their intermittent calling as they flit through the sky. Usually, when I hear them, I know that the duck will not be long in coming.

I have sometimes, when walking up, come upon snipe which have risen almost beneath my feet, and then so lethargically as to give me the easiest of shots. Often these are birds which have just completed a long coastal crossing in the early part of the autumn.

Methods of Shooting

Snipe are best shot on windy days, the line of guns walking into the wind, and taking the birds as they fight against the currents of air. Alternatively, they can be driven to a line of waiting guns, where they present the most sporting of shots. Once, whilst snipe-shooting on the west coast of Scotland, just as we had spread out to walk a section of inland marsh, I was surprised when our host discharged both barrels of his gun into the air. As we moved forward, keeping the line as straight as possible through the boggy ground, snipe were rising, well within range, at frequent intervals. Afterwards, this man explained to me that he always fired a couple of shots the moment he set foot on the marsh, for this served to make the birds lie close. On the day, he certainly proved his point, but I have tried it since, and found it to no avail. The main disadvantage, and my reluctance to make a regular practice of this, is that should there be any mallard or teal on the streams or pools, they will have been dispersed long before one is able to come within range of them.

Importance of Running Water

Possibly the rough-shooter, who has two or three acres of bog on his land, may find himself with virtually no snipe. If there is no running water this could be the answer, and there is not much one can do about it. If there is a stream, and still no snipe, then there is a deficiency in their feeding requirements. Their staple diet is worms, and these may be more in abundance in some marshes than others.

STERNEST CHALLENGE

The snipe and the woodcock both have an aura of mystery about them. Whence have they come? Nobody knows for sure, although our ornithologists have knowledge of most of the migratory flight-lines. They are the sternest challenge to any shooting man, testing his fieldcraft as well as his marksmanship. The beginner who learns to shoot them consistently in the early days of his shooting career will, in all probability, develop into a fine sportsman as he gains experience.

CHAPTER 18

Wildfowling

The wildfowler is part and parcel of folklore. To the layman, he is a legend, shrouded in mystery, and visualised as a hard gunning man, spending the majority of his life at the mercy of the tides in a flat bottomed punt, the measure of his success determining whether his family feeds or starves. Gnarled and weatherbeaten, barring accidents, he will live to a ripe old age, and recount his experiences of days gone by, in the local inn for the fee of a few pints of beer!

Wigeon

Photo: Calvin Williams

Whitefronted geese   Photo: Calvin Williams

THE MODERN WILDFOWLER

Yet, this is not the present-day wildfowler. This breed died out before the last war with the advent of more affluent times. The only "professional" today is he who receives payment in return for his services as a guide to those who shoot for sport alone. The Act which banned the sale of dead wild geese was surely only one of the nails hammered into the coffin of the "pro". Shortly before this Bill was passed, a fully grown Pinkfoot goose was fetching as little as twelve shillings. Considering they are the wiliest of all fowl, with a declining wintering population on the Wash, scant income could be expected from this species. Mallard, today, in the poulterers' shops are sold at about £1.50 each, or £2.75 per couple, so it would need a man of great marsh skills, constantly befriended by Lady Luck, to avert starvation.

The wildfowler today is purely a sportsman, in theory, anyway. It is a minority of "marsh cowboys" which, all too often, brings the sport into disrepute. The genuine fowler, though, is concerned with one thing only—the maximum amount of sport under the severest of conditions. His is no "fine weather" vocation. He has no specially sited stand, with game being systematically driven

159

over him, and shelter provided in case of a sudden storm. Instead, his only cover will be a deep dyke, with his feet constantly sinking into thick, black, oozing mud. Fine weather is no good to him. In fact, the fouler the weather, the better the fowling! Strong winds, blizzards and fog (the latter requiring an intimate knowledge of the terrain, supported by a *reliable* compass), are often the only conditions which will bring his quarry within gunshot.

OVERCROWDING ON THE MARSHES
No longer can he saunter on to the salt marshes, and make his way leisurely down to the mudflats, just as dawn is breaking, with ample time to find some cover. Today, all the ''best places'' are manned long before the first streaks of dawn appear in the eastern sky. Some ardent followers of their chosen sport are in position as early as 3 a.m. on a bitter winter's morning, just hoping for an odd shot in these lean times, when the fowl are far outnumbered by the fowlers.

A few years ago, I was talking to a veteran gunner of the Wash, a man who rarely missed a flight, morning and night. His best bag (geese) for one season, during the war years, was 160.

Coypu. Once a serious menace on the Wash

Photo: Guy Smith

160

Birds for the table. Canada goose weighing 8¼ lb., Mallard weighing 3¼ lb.
Photo: Calvin Williams

Certainly, a handy supplement in times of rationing! In 1968 he rulled off his "log-book" on 20th February at 27. In 1971 he managed only five! This, surely, is an indication of how times have changed.

The causes are many. Modern means of transport are bringing people to the Wash (the finest wintering ground for Pinkfeet geese in England), whereas, years ago, they would have contented themselves with shooting duck on their local rivers. Increased shooting can only serve to make the quarry more wary. Certainly, fewer birds are shot today than in the past. They have learned to seek quieter refuges. The reclaiming of large tracts of land from the sea is depriving them of a natural habitat, as well as food, in the case of the wigeon which has gone elsewhere in search of its beloved *zos*.

The modern fowler comes from all walks of life. He may be a company director, or from the shop-floor of some factory. There is no class distinction on the saltmarshes. Each is governed by the written, and unwritten, laws of wildfowling. The individual skills of one may be superior to another, and Lady Luck is impartial with her favours.

TOO MUCH LEGISLATION

Fowling today cannot, by any stretch of imagination, be either lucrative or remunerative. A bird for one's own table is the most one can expect and, furthermore, it will be appreciated. Legislation is playing a large part in the sport, nowadays, serving only to stifle individuality. The nature of a foray is no longer at the discretion of the wildfowler himself. The acquisition of a permit is necessary before he can legally carry a gun down to the sea-wall, and even when he has crossed to the "spike grass" he is still restricted by boundaries which never existed hitherto.

All this, for good or evil, has moulded the wildfowler of the eighties. This is why one may pass him in the crowded streets of a large town, and dismiss him as just another "man of the street". The legend has been replaced by its modern counterpart.

CLOTHING AND EQUIPMENT

However, before we set foot on the marshes some thought to the type of clothing and equipment needed are advisable. Not only our personal comfort, but our very lives may depend upon our choice.

Waterproofs are an essential. However, it is no good buying cheap ones. They must be both durable and *comfortable,* for shooting will be under the most difficult conditions. My own preference is for thornproofs, and one such jacket, treated annually with a waterproofing substance, lasted me eleven years. Large spacious pockets are advisable for cartridges. Cartridge-belts are rather exposed to the elements whilst wildfowling, and I have found that even when using the modern plastic-cased cartridges they are inclined to slip out and become lost. With prices as they are today, wastage is inexcusable.

Waders (thigh-length) are advisable, not only for crossing deep creeks, but also for kneeling in the mud. They are far preferable to waterproof trousers, and much more comfortable.

I make no excuse for returning to the subject of guns and cartridges once more. The choice where wildfowling is concerned determines the difference between wounded birds dying a lingering death far out on the mudflats, and finishing up in the bag. Judgement of range in open spaces such as coastal marshes is not easy, and most of the shots will be taken at long range anyway. A 3-inch chambered 12-bore is adequate for most types of wildfowling. Often the beginner, if he can afford it, is tempted to invest in one of the larger bores. It just is not worth it. They are cumbersome and heavy to carry, and difficult to swing on to a target, especially if you have had to carry it two or three miles across the marsh beforehand.

There is much controversy regarding shot-sizes. The fallacy that the larger the shot, the farther it will kill, will exist for evermore. Admittedly, a lucky pellet will often bring down a duck or goose at extreme range, but it is the *pattern* of shot which counts. Buckshot sizes (SG, SSG, AAA, etc.) throw little or no pattern, whatsoever, and a goose at 40 yards is much more likely to be missed than killed. Likewise, small shot such as Nos. 5 or 6 will only maim. A happy medium must be found. The majority of my own geese have been killed with BB or No. 1. I would recommend these shot sizes to all who pursue geese.

Of course, if one carried all the equipment recommended in various journals and books, one would be so weighed down that the sport would become irksome. Therefore, one must determine which items are *essential*. The terrain over which one shoots is the best guide to this. For instance, if you are only going to stand on the sea-wall to shoot at flight times, then waders will be totally unnecessary. As in most walks of life, common-sense predominates in wildfowling.

DANGERS OF THE MARSHES

Mostly the dangers of the marshes are under-rated. Often visitors prefer to view these places from the comparative comfort of the sea-wall. However, there are always the more adventurous among the community who desire to go and "find out" for themselves, and it is for the benefit of these people that this section has been written.

First, we must remember that tides are always unpredictable. One may set out, walking seawards, content in the knowledge that the tide will not flow for at least another 1½–2 hours. However, a strong breeze suddenly strengthens, and in a matter of a quarter of an hour, a gale is blowing. Still undaunted, one carries on, noticing that the incoming sea is still some distance away. The unwary walker has overlooked his greatest danger, though, in the form of the creeks which zig-zag across the saltings. This is where his deadliest peril lies. The incoming tide will creep, unnoticed, through these, filling them, silently and rapidly. The retreat back to the mainland is cut off. Where, a short time ago, it was possible either to jump a narrow channel of water, or else, with wellington boots, to wade through a depth of only inches, one is now confronted with a swirling current of several feet. At the very least, a soaking will follow. Therefore, one is well advised to start back at once if the wind begins increasing in force to any great extent.

A permanent danger, throughout all seasons of the year, is a combination of thick mud and quicksands. Mud in itself is treacherous. Although it may not be sufficient to suck one down beneath its surface, it is capable of impeding one's progress to such an extent that one may not be successful in reaching the mainland ahead of the incoming tide. Quicksands, however, are a different proposition, altogether. They move, and change position from one week to the next. There is virtually no way of telling their whereabouts, except that they are unlikely to be found on the saltings, restricting themselves to the mudflats.

However, should one be unfortunate enough to step into one of these patches of moving, sucking mud, it is most important not to struggle, and to avoid panicking. One must lie down on one's back, and attempt to ease oneself slowly out of the danger area. If a companion is nearby, he must take care not to find himself in the same predicament and, from a distance, offer aid in the form of a long stick or a piece of rope or, if neither of these are readily available, then items of clothing tied together, will suffice.

Probably the greatest danger of all, complimentary to both quicksands and fast flowing tides, is a sudden sea-mist. There is no knowing where these will rise, but they are more prevalent on still, damp days, during winter, than at any other time. The grey vapour will erase every landmark from view within a matter of minutes, and the stranger may well find himself walking out to sea when he fully believes himself to be heading back towards the mainland! There is only one way to combat this danger, and that is by carrying a small pocket-compass at all times. These are inexpensive to buy, in fact, very cheap when one considers that they may be a major factor in saving one's life. One must learn, however, the correct method of using them, taking a bearing before setting out, otherwise they will be useless when the whole landscape has been obscured by fog.

WHEN IN DOUBT, HIRE A GUIDE

These are only a few of the ways in which the perils of the wildfowler may be combated. The only real safe manner in which these wild and beautiful places may be explored safely is to enlist the help of a local "guide". However, even then, one must be sure that the man is bona-fide, and not somebody just wishing to earn some easy money, trusting to luck that his judgement will be correct.

These marshes are not to be trifled with. Death is ever present amid a wild chorus of sea birds, and the gentle murmur of the sea, as it laps at the stalk edges. It is a merciless place engendering an atmosphere of false security at times, when the foolish and the unwary must pay the price.

B.A.S.C.

Every wildfowler should belong to the British Association for Shooting and Conservation, formerly the Wildfowlers' Association of Great Britain and Ireland. In these uncertain times when field sports are constantly under threat from a number of sources, **strength is in unity**, and this particular association has done much to ensure the safety of sport. Yet, we can never afford to relax our vigilance.

The B.A.S.C. covers just about every aspect of the sport, issuing a quarterly magazine which keeps members informed, as well as publishing a variety of booklets for the beginner.

LEARN TO IDENTIFY THE QUARRY

No fowler should set foot on the foreshore unless he can positively identify the quarry which he pursues. Many of the species are protected, for example Brent geese and shelduck. He who shoots one of these birds faces a severe penalty. A booklet entitled *Know Your Quarry* is published by the B.A.S.C. illustrating the various species, and is an invaluable guide for the amateur. However, it is important that the reader learns to study his wildfowl, and it is hoped that the following information will give him some insight into the habits of a few of the birds which he will invariably encounter. The aim is not simply to learn to shoot them. An interest in wildfowling goes much deeper than that. We are conservationists, having a deep respect for the fowl which we pursue. We are hungry for knowledge. Where and why do birds flight at certain times? On what do they feed? Are they migratory?

Only one thing is certain. We shall never stop learning.

MALLARD

The mallard is a greedy bird, surpassed in this only by its distant cousin the farmyard duck. It has little thought for anything else except its love of food. From August onwards it will flight in at dusk to the stubble fields, spending the nocturnal hours in search of the grain which has eluded the combine-harvester. Nowadays, though, with modern farming methods its time on the stubble is limited. Within a few days of the harvest being completed, the stubble burning will begin, and then the plough will transform those golden acres of but a week ago, into newly turned earth. The mallard must search elsewhere.

Soon the potato crop will be lifted, and another supply of food is available to the mallard. Careless pickers will provide this duck with a gluttonous feast. Perhaps the duck will have a full month's feeding ahead of them, depending on the eagerness of the farmer to plough the land, but what then?

From November onwards the mallard is hunting far and wide for its food. One particular favourite with this bird is the acorn, a delicacy which it shares with the pheasant. Of course, the shooting man provides the mallard with valuable food during times of hard weather, in the form of flight ponds fed with barley and maize.

By day the coastal mallard rests far out on the mudflats. This is an ideal habitat, providing it with a refuge, its only danger being the guns which await the night and morning flights on the sea walls. It has sharp eyesight, yet all too often its cunning is hampered by its greed. A quiet pond that contains an ample supply of grain is an incentive to this bird to drop into feed, often without circling to ascertain that no concealed gunner lies in wait. Mallard which have survived a duck shoot will avoid that particular stretch of water for perhaps a fortnight, but they still remember that food is to be found there, and in due course they will return.

One of the major problems, and something which is detrimental to any species of wildlife is an abundance of males. One has only to visit a recreational park where mallard swim on a pool, and it will at once be obvious that the drakes outnumber the ducks by about five to one. The only answer is to thin out the drakes by shooting. From March onwards drakes will be fighting furiously over the ducks, and this is not conducive to good breeding.

When it comes to building a nest, the duck mallard shows unbelievable stupidity. Many conservationists provide nesting baskets for mallard on inland waters, and this at least ensures protection from foxes and other ground vermin. Strangely, duck are attracted towards Reynard, and will often swim alongside the bank of a pool or river, quacking and mocking him. It was this curiosity which led to their capture in days of old when the dogs of the decoymen used to lead their quarry into the decoy pipes.

Of course, our resident mallard population is swelled during the winter months by migrant birds. Extensive ringing has proved beyond doubt that duck have travelled to Britain from as far afield as the steppes of Russia. Nowadays, the decoys of old are put to a use that is in the interests of the birds themselves. The trapped duck, instead of finding themselves en route to the nearest market, are ringed and then given their freedom.

TEAL

The teal is the smallest of our native wild duck, and is to be found throughout the British Isles. The cock (not the 'drake') is easily recognised by the dark brown markings on its head, whilst the female is less glamorous, resembling a much smaller version of the mallard duck.

The habits of the teal are very similar to those of its larger cousin, feeding out on the mudflats by day, and flighting in to roost on some quiet inland pool at dusk. From November onwards, teal are often seen flying in bunches of twenty or more, their numbers swelled by those which have just arrived on our shores. Sometimes, the layman mistakes them for wigeon, but their shrill piping whistle is very different from the constant 'whee-oo' of the wigeon; two or three notes, and then silence. Their wingbeats, too, are light, and scarcely audible.

The teal is far more wary than the mallard, and its cunning is surpassed only by the wigeon. At the slightest sound it will be on the wing, its steep rise and sheer speed alone often defeating the stalking gunner. It also has a habit of submerging itself for long periods with only the tip of its beak showing above water level, and many wounded birds have successfully evaded searching gundogs with this ploy.

The teal is not the greedy feeder which almost every other species of wild duck are. It is fond of grain, but seldom will it go 'stubbling' at harvest time. Fresh water streams will provide it with a variety of water weed, and the author recently examined the crop of a dead bird, and found that it had been feeding almost entirely on algae, that dark green weed which grows prolifically on stagnant water, giving the appearance of thick slime. Although teal will feed alongside mallard and wigeon, these birds seem to tolerate each other rather than integrate.

Teal need not, by necessity, flight inland to feed, for they are, unlike mallard, content to fill their crops with the seeds of marsh samphire. However, it is possibly a change of diet which prompts them to fly shorewards. Their favourite menu at a fresh water stream or pool being the seeds of the common spike rushes, or buttercup seeds on a flooded meadow.

Most of the teal wintering in this country come from the countries around the Baltic, or even further east. Recent experiments in the ringing of these birds have proved this beyond doubt. A few remain behind in the spring to breed along with our resident birds.

This small duck is regarded as a worthwhile quarry by most sportsmen, for its speed and cunning render it the most elusive of targets. It may spring up at the most unexpected moment from a creek on the mudflats, utilising the element of surprise, or materialise suddenly out of the gathering darkness as it crosses the sea wall; its high-pitched piping mocking the unwary gunner as it speeds inland to some quiet pool or stream. Our marshes would be lacking, indeed, without the presence of the teal.

WIGEON

The wigeon rivals the teal in being the most wary, as well as the most sporting, of all our wild duck. Very seldom is the wigeon seen singly, for it is fond of the company of its own species, and once I remember seeing raft upon raft of these birds on the River Welland, one November morning, just as dawn was breaking. At a rough estimation I would be prepared to quote a figure of some 2,000, feeling that this was probably well below the true total.

The wigeon is not often seen by the inland dweller, except in times of very rough weather, when they are forced to seek the shelter of rivers and lakes. They feed by night, and roost by day, perhaps only altering this routine when the winter is severe, and they must feed where and when they are able. They are a worthy quarry for any true sportsman, and a 'right and left', secured in the half light of either dawn or dusk, is no mean task.

CURLEW*

The curlew is a winter visitor to our coastal areas, spending much of the spring and summer months inland, breeding on rivers, lakes and often on desolate moorland. It is a strange sensation, indeed, to one who is familiar with the coast, to be possibly a hundred miles or so inland, on a warm summer's day, and suddenly to hear that wonderful warble which defies description.

Curlew return to the coast during late July or August, bringing their offspring with them. They have only a few weeks of safety left, for come September 1st, they become a legitimate quarry for the wildfowler. They must rely on their cunning, as well as that sudden jinking swerve, employed at the first sign of danger, if they are to survive the winter.

These birds are not just shot because they present a challenging target, with their irregular pattern of flight, but also because they are edible, and extremely palatable, in the early autumn. This is when they are feeding on the stubble fields, close to the sea wall, but once these are ploughed in, and they are forced to find their food on the seaward side of the boundary, their flesh becomes bitter, and unfit for the table. If stuffed with sage and onions, and roasted slowly, the flavour is very similar to that of the mallard, and sometimes almost indiscernible from

NB: The curlew is now a protected species. See Appendix.

it. The breast is virtually the only part worth eating, there being enough meat here to satisfy the average person at one meal.

The curlew is a gregarious bird, usually to be found feeding and roosting in numbers, the official term of which is a 'herd'. It is fascinating to listen to them from any of the sea walls which border agricultural areas. Whilst feeding they are comparatively silent, more intent on eating than conversing with each other, but about a quarter of an hour or so before they are due to flight back to their roosts out on the mudflats, the air is filled with a chorus so wild and wonderful that no musical instrument could ever hope to compete with it.

Suddenly, silence reigns once more, and the hidden listener might be forgiven for thinking that the birds in question have departed in the opposite direction. However, a swish of wings overhead assures him that this is not the case, as the first bunch of curlew lead the way homewards. Perhaps the observer is not so well hidden as he thinks, and the dozen or so birds see him, their shrill warning cry and change of direction giving away his position to those following behind. The remainder of the herd will cross well wide of him.

The curlew is fortunate in that, except during the early part of the shooting season, before the migrant duck and geese have arrived, he will often be allowed to pass to and fro without being fired at, the waiting gunners reluctant to 'waste' powder and shot on him. Nevertheless, he is the wariest bird on the marshes, and even with the present-day influx of irresponsible shooters, he will survive, winter after winter, whilst other species are reduced to an alarmingly low resident population, or else driven away altogether.

MOORHEN

There are few of us who have not, at some time or other, met up with that inquisitive little bird, the moorhen. We may have seen it darting through the reed beds or saltings, or swimming with that so familiar jerking movement on canal or recreation park lake. The moorhen is ubiquitous. Wherever there is water, it will abound.

Although reasonably tame, our approach will at once be heralded by a loud unmistakable 'chirrup', as it gives warning of the coming of Man. This bird itself will skulk in the rushes until the danger is past, and it is capable of remaining for long periods under water.

It is a strange bird, and reminiscent of the pheasant in many ways. It likes thick hedgerows on marshy ground, and roosts not in the reeds, but in the branches of some thick bush which affords it protection from ground and winged vermin. Although a strong flier, it prefers to run when danger threatens on land, and possibly this is the reason why it had never been classed as a sporting bird, even though its dark meat is very palatable.

In the spring it will make its nest in the reeds of a brook or dyke, although sometimes it chooses the thick branches of that bush in which it has roosted throughout the winter months. Occasionally, it will not bother to construct its own nest, but will occupy one that has been built the previous year by a pigeon or a crow. Just as the moorhen itself makes good eating, so do its eggs, although hard-boiling is advised as they will have absorbed a variety of germs, particularly if the nest is situated in a muddy stream.

Seldom will one find a moorhen's nest that has been robbed of its eggs by either rats or winged predators. Certainly they are palatable, but one theory has it that when danger threatens, the bird makes a terrific splashing, drenching the attacker. This explanation I find difficult to believe, for were this the case, then surely mallard nests would go untouched as this duck adopts the same means of defence. Perhaps this is one of Nature's own secrets which she is unwilling to reveal.

A hard winter is the moorhen's greatest enemy. Unlike other fowl which fly for miles in search of open water, possibly even to the coast, the moorhen remains on the ice, and in the frozen brooks, searching for any gleanings. They are easy prey for the fox, and should the ice persist for more than a week or so, their numbers will be drastically reduced.

Whilst on the subject of moorhens, we must not forget their larger cousin, the coot. Although not so numerous, the coot is easily recognisable by its larger size. It prefers larger tracts of water, and will often spend the daylight hours resting far from the reach of its enemies.

Perhaps both species are taken for granted, and we are inclined to dismiss them when viewing a flock of waterfowl on an expanse of water. Yet, they are part and parcel of the interesting wildlife which exists on our marshes, rivers, and pools. They breed prolifically, and their only enemies are rats and foxes when they venture ashore. Often, they are detrimental to wildfowl reserves and flight-ponds, greedily devouring the grain which has been tipped into the shallows for mallard.

However, many of our waters would seem deserted if it was not for the moorhen and the coot. They are all part of Nature's plan.

CANADA GEESE

The Canada Goose, unfortunately, enjoys a much lower status in this country than its migratory cousins, the Greylag, the Pinkfoot and the Whitefront. Whilst sportsmen spend their leisure time during the winter months, often lying for hours in freezing mud, in pursuit of *wild* geese, the Canada is often allowed to pass by unshot at, and is considered to be of a very inferior quality.

Yet, the Canada goose is often only 'tame' when in surroundings, such as a pleasure park, where it knows it is safe from interference. Once it flights from here, it is wily, and its instincts are tuned to self-preservation.

There are many advantages in treating the Canada as a sporting bird. It can, of course, be shot legally, and often is, but without the glamour attached to true wildfowling. Its eating qualities, in my opinion, are far in excess of any of the species, including domestic geese. I once shot one weighing 14 lbs (627 g), providing my family with some very tasty and economical meals.

Canada geese do much damage to growing crops, and very often they are shot out of season, between February 1st and August 31st, by irate farmers. This being the case, surely it would be preferable to see them as a 'recognised' quarry for sportsmen, throughout the winter months, when their numbers could easily be controlled in this way.

Often, in coastal areas, Canada geese will roost out on the mud-flats, taking care to keep well apart from the grey geese. There is a resident skein of about seventy of these on the Solway Firth, which flight daily between the shore and a large inland lake. Sometimes, a few get shot. I saw four fall to a burst from a 5-shot automatic one early September morning, but, thereafter, they took good care to keep out of gunshot.

There is a similar flock of Canadas at Wells-next-the-Sea in Norfolk which have also learnt to look after themselves.

However, we must remember that, in its native country, the Canada goose is the wiliest of all wild geese, anywhere in the world. It heads the sporting list, in fact. It is only its association with park lakes and boating pools, where visitors are able to feed it that has lowered its status. Away from this environment, and once fully aware that it is likely to be shot at, its reflexes are sharpened, and it becomes a quarry worthy of any wildfowler.

BUILDING UP AN INLAND WILDFOWL SHOOT

Wildfowl Instead of Pheasants

Far too many rough shoots today concentrate solely on pheasants. In the majority of areas this bird is regarded as the epitome of sport. This is fine, except in places where the terrain is not conducive to pheasants, and as a result much hard work and cash is expended in return for meagre, often poor, results. But the tenants and syndicates persist, year after year, and whilst we can only admire their perseverance in many ways, a change of direction would probably benefit their pockets and their sport. There are few shoots which could not be turned into excellent wildfowl shoots with a little forethought.

171

First, let us consider those shoots which are not generally acceptable to pheasants. Discounting grouse-moors, we are left with upland areas, probably much of the ground being planted with coniferous trees. It is a fallacy that such places are attractive to pheasants, for beneath these closely planted, sometimes impenetrable coverts, there is little or no food to be found for the birds, and generally the ground is devoid of undergrowth due to the branches preventing the sunlight from filtering through. Unless some adjoining arable land is rented, and in hilly areas the farms are mostly devoted to grazing land with possibly the odd field of winter fodder, then generally the pheasants will remain in the valleys below. They prefer the warmer climate as well as a greater abundance of food. It is possible sometimes to hold them on your upland shoot in the early part of the season by regular feeding, but once the cold weather sets in they will begin to stray down to the lower slopes.

It is frustrating for the small shoot owner, who has painstakingly reared a hundred or so birds throughout the summer, to find suddenly, with the advent of November, when shooting should be at its best, that all his birds have deserted him. They may return briefly during a mild spell, but a large percentage of them will be shot on neighbouring land. The author knows, because it has happened to him, and this is one of the main reasons (apart from a love of wildfowling) why he is now 'thinking wildfowl'.

The reader will at once say 'but I have little or no water on my land', but I urge him to bear with me a little longer. Very few shoots of any size are completely devoid of a pool or a stream of some sort, and even if the land is totally dry then there are ways and means of attracting duck.

Artificial Flight Ponds

First, let us consider the improvements that can be made to any small tract of water, and I would stress here that often very small pools can be turned into flight-ponds with regular feeding. Mallard are greedy, and will travel miles to a place where they know there is an abundance of barley. So start feeding that tiny pool which up until now you have disregarded, and be patient. I waited two seasons for such a pond to develop its full potential, and now it averages thirty birds a year.

A flight-pond can always be constructed along a stream simply by widening one bank, and building a dam downstream so that the water fills the newly excavated area before flowing on its former course. But do make sure that your landlord is in agreement with what you are doing. It may be necessary to stop the flow of water for a few days whilst your pool fills up, and someone lower down might be wondering why his cattle-drink has suddenly run dry!

The best time to start work on any new pool is in the spring. This will give the excavations time to settle and assume a 'natural' look before the next season. Likewise, in the event of a summer drought, it may be well into October before your pool has any water in it, and you will have missed the best part of the shooting.

Of course, you may well have to start building your pools from scratch, and in a way this is preferable because you can site them just where you want them. One important factor at the outset is to discover whether or not the land will hold water, and your best method of determining this is to dig a hole, approximately a yard square (1 m) and a foot (30.5 cm) deep, on the site of your proposed pool and see whether it fills up during a couple of weeks of rainfall. If the water is soaking away, then you will need to line the bottom of the pool with a sheet of heavy duty PVC, obtainable from most farm suppliers, as this material is used in the protection of hayricks.

A JCB will make short work of the excavations. Remember, though, a duck pool needs to be shallow, no more than a couple of feet in the deepest part, for duck like to dabble. Use the soil which you dig out to line your banks.

The next stage is to line the base of your pool with the PVC. Take care that there are no sharp stones beneath it which will puncture it, and you may save yourself a lot of hard work by lining it with a layer of sand before unrolling the artificial base.

A calm day is best, otherwise the PVC will billow in the wind as you unroll it, and you might accidentally rip it. Weight it down with soil, again taking care to see that you do not throw stones or rocks on to it, and then cover it lightly with soil. Do not walk about on it afterwards, and if there are sheep or cattle in the vicinity, then fence it off. One animal wandering into it will ruin all your hard work, and a punctured base is almost impossible to repair. You will have to invest in another area of PVC, and go to all the trouble of laying it again!

The pool needs to be as natural-looking as possible. This is easily achieved by planting reeds around the edge, and the addition of one or two willow trees will be added cover in the years that lie ahead. A bare pool in the middle of a field means that wildfowl resting there during the daytime will be virtually unapproachable, and, anyway, they prefer using pools which have plenty of cover.

If the pool is a large one then it will be to your advantage to build an island in the centre with some nesting baskets on it, and/or have a raft for this purpose as well. However, if it is your intention to have duck breeding on the pool, be sure in the first place that it is free from interference. If there is any likelihood of hooligans visiting the place during your absence then it will be preferable for both you and the ducks if the birds breed elsewhere.

So far we have only discussed the prospect of making one pool, but if you have an acreage of any size, and are really intent on substituting your pheasants with mallard, then you will almost certainly need more than that. One pool can really only be shot once a fortnight, so more than one is needed to provide a regular weekly shoot. 500 acres of land should be able to accommodate half-a-dozen flight-ponds quite easily.

Siting is of paramount importance. Where possible avoid building pools close to your boundaries. At this stage you may get on very well with your neighbours, but shoots have an annoying habit of changing hands, and you could find yourself with a bunch of unscrupulous neighbours who, quite legitimately, stand on their own land and flight your duck, not only shooting your birds, but ruining your pool with over-shooting.

Likewise, the pools must be sufficiently far apart so that you can shoot them without disturbing the others. As a guide, you should aim at having a minimum distance of a quarter of a mile between each pond. Do not be tempted on shooting days to divide your guns up so that several pools are covered. Birds which have escaped a barrage need somewhere to rest in peace for the night and, if possible, you want them to do that on *your* land. Shoot your ponds in rotation, taking the good with the bad, and do not be tempted to return to one pool a few nights later just because the duck are using it again.

Feeding

Feeding is the most important factor for the continuance of good sport. Mallard are greedy, and they love barley, but if you have an abundance of moorhens these birds will devour the grain before the wildfowl flight in. There is a simple remedy for this. **Use whole maize** for the smaller birds will not be able to devour it.

Rotten potatoes are also very acceptable to duck. If this type of food is required for immediate use, then unless the tubers are well rotted, they will need to be boiled. It is a good idea to dump several hundredweight of these in the water early in the season and let them rot down naturally so that the mallard will feed on them once the frosts begin. A frozen pool does not always mean an absence of duck. In many cases potatoes heaped well above the surface, even when the pool is frozen, will entice duck to drop in to feed.

One of the best lures for mallard is **rotten bananas**. Of course, they are not always easy to come by, but if you know a fruiterer you can mention to him that you are interested in taking any off his hands that are unfit for human consumption. The author once experimented with a couple of bags of these and the duck poured into the pool at dusk as though word had got round the district!

It is best to feed a little and often, that is daily. Too much grain lying in the water will attract rats, and you may be puzzled because your feed is being taken but no duck are flighting in. The best time to feed is an hour or so before dusk. In that way you will not disturb any duck which are using the pool as a day time roost, and you will also ensure that the grain is not devoured by either rats or moorhens before the duck find it.

Rear a Few Duck

Of course, conservation must be uppermost in your mind. By changing your shooting policy it does not mean that you have escaped the labours of rearing. If you shoot duck in any quantity then you must endeavour to replace these birds.

Rearing duck is far easier and far cheaper than rearing pheasants. If you buy a hundred day–olds then you will release a far higher percentage of birds into the wild. I quote one example of one year when I found a mallard's nest in a dangerous place, and I took the ten eggs and put them under a broody hen. I was successful in releasing ten birds back into the pool!

So, having built pools and reared your ducks, you must concentrate on your keepering duties much the same as you did previously where pheasants were concerned. Foxes and crows are your worst enemies. Wage continued war on them, as well as taking steps to ensure that rats do not move into the area surrounding your pools.

In America some 'duck hunters' use artificial pools, and purely out of curiosity I have used these and found them to be very effective. They comprise of a large sheet of clear polythene, cut to an irregular shape, laid out on the ground and weighted down by rocks and soil around the edges. With one or two decoys placed on it, it looks the genuine thing to birds passing over. Sometimes one does not even need to use a call. Nevertheless, it is too artificial for regular use and you will not be able to lure birds to it frequently, merely taking toll of passing ducks.

Moonlight Shooting is Detrimental to Flight-ponds

A sportsman may well find that he has no regular flight-lines over his shoot, but it is not absolutely necessary to have these. I have shot duck for the past decade on a pool situated above 1,000 feet (304.8 m) in the heart of a Forestry Commission wood, and simply by feeding regularly I have lured the birds there. The secret, of course, is to shoot sparingly, and I never stop on until it is absolutely dark. I am always pleased to hear birds still circling as I creep away, more than satisfied with the brace which I have in the bag.

Moonlight shooting is almost always detrimental to any inland shoot, and should be reserved only for coastal marshes. Duck are far more easily disturbed under the moon, and again I quote a personal experience which it is hoped that the reader will benefit from. At the time I was renting an exceptionally good flight–pond, close to the industrial Midlands, which was yielding something in the region of seventy birds per season. One night I decided upon a moonlit foray, and after a lengthy stalk I managed to creep within range of my pool. There were about forty duck feeding on it, and as they jumped I took a 'right and left'. I felt very satisfied with myself as I returned home shortly after midnight, but I was to pay the penalty for my nocturnal excursion. Mallard had been flighting in nightly in numbers all season, but after that I did not see a single duck for almost a month!

It is not sufficient simply to feed and shoot a pool. Constant observation is necessary, and one must be prepared to devote a number of nights each week to watching the pools from a distance with a pair of binoculars. Note the number of birds, count them nightly, and if their numbers diminish take steps to find out why. There may be a variety of reasons. Often in September the mallard are away stubbling, but there is a mystery in my own part of the hills which I have not yet solved, after fifteen years of trying. I never see any duck on my pools during November. Obviously this has something to do with their feeding habits, for no amount of barley or potatoes will tempt them to return before the first week in December.

Poachers Must Be Deterred

Also, by constant vigilance you will deter poachers. Poaching is far more detrimental to a duck shoot than it is to a pheasant covert. It is not the amount of birds shot which will deprive you of sport, but the *disturbance* which will drive the duck away for lengthy periods.

Of course, mallard will provide the nucleus of your sport, but most pools will yield the odd teal from time to time. Sometimes, on a larger stretch of water, there will be the additional bonus of wigeon, shoveler, and pintail. One other welcome visitor, particularly if the pool is situated in a wooded area, will be woodcock. These delightful, mysterious long–billed birds, the most testing of all shots, use my pools regularly, and during observation sessions I have seen them alight amongst the heaps of rotting potatoes. I can only conclude that they find some grubs and insects amongst the tubers which are a delicacy to them.

Water is an asset to any shoot, but if your pheasant programme is not working out then change over to duck. There is untold satisfaction to be gained from building up a successful wildfowl shoot where previously few wildfowl were encountered.

FIRST SOLWAY GOOSE OF THE SEASON

It is now many years ago since I first set foot on the shores of the Solway Firth. I will never forget that first visit, so indelibly is it imprinted on my mind, for it was responsible for calling me back there, year after year, and instilling in me a deep love for that wild and desolate place, with Criffel looming up in the background.

I think my greatest moment of triumph, apart from the shooting of my first goose, came about ten years ago. The weather had been mild all week, so far removed from the traditional gales which every wildfowler prays for, that I had resigned myself to enjoying the peace and solitude without raising my hopes of securing a goose. It is at such times as these that the unexpected usually happens.

I was on Priestside merse on the morning in question. I had watched skein after skein of Pinkfeet geese, leaving the sands, three or four gunshots high by the time they reached the first line of guns at Powhillon. I sat on the grass, watching, making no effort at concealment for I had long since given up any hope of a shot. Suddenly, I heard geese, and not so very far away.

First Solway Goose of the season

Photo: Guy Smith

177

Hastily, I dropped into a nearby creek where I crouched, watching and waiting. Seconds later, three geese came into view over the tall hawthorn hedge which separated the farm from the merse. They were flying low, and wheeling round in my direction. I could hardly believe my luck. I was the only fowler on Priestside, the others having congregated at Powhillon, or else remained in bed, on account of the calm weather, so the three geese came on towards me, without having a shot fired at them. I should have had a ''right and left'' easily, but it was probably the unexpectedness of their appearance, and my own nervous excitement, which caused me to miss with the first barrel, and score with the second. Little did I realise, as my yellow labrador, Remus, retrieved that bird, that I had shot the first goose of the season on the Solway. Consequently, that Pinkfoot was photographed many times before it finally appeared on the table!

I have had some bitter disappointments on the Solway as well as my moments of triumph, days when one asks oneself whether it is all really worth it, but knowing full well that it is. I had the frustrating experience one morning of dropping a goose on to the sands in front of me, and chasing it for a full mile, my quarry managing to keep a full gunshot's distance in front of me, until finally it gained the ebbing tide where I managed to shoot it, but lost it. Then there was the evening when I killed a goose stone dead—dropping it on the opposite side of the Lochar Water. It lay there, only yards away, and I cursed myself for having left Remus at the hotel rather than submitting him to a wait of several hours in pouring rain. The sticky mud of the Lochar prevented me from making the crossing, even though the depth of water would have allowed me to do so. I had no alternative other than to leave it where it was.

Places to Visit Around the Solway
I find time for activities other than wildfowling during my annual week on the Solway. There are many attractive places well worth a visit within easy motoring distance of Dumfries. Kippford is a delightful little village, but my favourite is Southerness, with its lighthouse and rocky beach. It has the true flavour of the wildness of the west coast of Scotland, and it is easy to conjure up visions of the days of Paul Jones. I also enjoy the festivities of Haloween night—something which is mostly passed over, almost forgotten, south of the border.

In spite of the changing times, I shall still continue to visit the Solway. It has too great a hold over me for me to be able to

Solway Marshes

Photo: Guy Smith

relinquish it, and I shall return there year after year, as though some invisible force is willing me to do so, in the same way that the vast hordes of wild geese return to winter on the Solway mudflats each autumn.

COLONEL PETER HAWKER

No chapter on wildfowling would be complete without some reference to the late Colonel Peter Hawker, often referred to as 'the grandfather of wildfowling'. This man has become a legend, and in spite of the advance of technology over the 128 years since his death, few, if any of us, could equal his marksmanship or his knowledge of the quarry.

Colonel Peter Hawker, son of Colonel Peter Rynes Hawker was born on December 24th 1786. Had it not been for a stray musket ball which lodged itself in his thigh at the battle of Talavera on July 28th 1809, it is probable that little would have been known about this very singular man. As it was, fate decreed that Peter Hawker, junior, was to become one of the finest sportsmen ever to set forth with a gun under his arm and a dog at his heels, and to write one of the best instructional works on the subject ever to be published. This book, *Instructions to Young Sportsmen in all that Relates to Guns and Shooting* was revised in nine editions by the author, and the tenth was nearing completion at the time of his death in 1853. However, it was his *Diaries*, religiously written since 1802, which really serve to give us an insight into the character of the man; these latter being edited and published by Sir Ralph Payne-Gallway in 1893, some forty years after Hawker's death.

However, Peter Hawker was, first and foremost, a soldier, following in the footsteps of his father. He was gazetted cornet to the First Royal Dragoons in 1803, obtained his troop in 1804, and served with his regiment in Spain under Wellington in 1808–9. Here he won for his regiment the first honour 'Douro' on their colours, before receiving that fateful musket wound in his thigh. For the next four years he underwent a series of operations, but in 1813 he was compelled to resign his commission, and was invalided out of the British Army. A devastating blow, indeed, for one so dedicated to a military way of life, and Hawker was very bitter about this decision over which he had no control. Even the fact that he was a close friend of the Duke of Clarence, later to be crowned King William IV, could not save him, and within a few months he was back in the family home at Longparish.

Now Hawker began the life of a country gentleman, devoted primarily to his shooting and fishing, with his love of music coming a close second. In between these pursuits he found time to travel abroad, a luxury denied to all but the very wealthy in those days. In the spring of 1819 he visited Paris, followed by a tour of France, lasting seventy-one days, in the autumn. In 1822 he visited Belgium, and Rouen and Paris again in 1828. The year 1835 found him in Jersey and Guernsey, and in 1841 he returned to France, staying for some weeks at Boulogne, Abbeyville and Paris. In 1844 he completed a short tour of Germany. Amidst his chronicles of shooting and fishing he also wrote of these travels, and one note sums up his opinion of foreigners.

suffice to say that from the instant you enter Dover until you have got safely clear of your hotel in Paris, you have to guard against one incessant attack of the grossest imposition.

On his return to Paris in 1828, Hawker noted the changes which had taken place since his last visit.

Every article dearer than it was, but now the French have a fixed price, and you have not to bargain like a Jew to avoid being cheated. The wines are decidedly not so good as in former times, and you still have the same difficulty in getting a good sized glass to drink out of — French opera much improved, but Italian opera fallen off.

Hawker again returned to the Continent in July 1841, and was incensed by the fact that the carriage in which he travelled from Boulogne to Paris took twenty-one hours to complete the distance of 140 miles. His last journey abroad was to Germany in September 1844; apart from his military travels abroad, he saw much of foreign countries. However, he had objects other than mere sight-seeing when travelling; a vague mention is made in his diaries of the business he transacted in introducing to the attention of musicians his patent hand-moulds (a device enabling the scales to be played mechanically on a piano), though we hear nothing of the results of placing them on the market. Music played a greater part in his life than we are apt to think, as can be surmised from a brief entry in his chronicles. In September 1837 he shoots on the 1st, 2nd, 4th, 6th, 9th, 11th, 12th, 13th and 15th, and on the 16th he attends:

an exquisite musical treat - Thalberg at Winchester with More, Albertazzi and others. It seemed like a romance to have such gods amongst the Hampshire hogs!

There is little reference in his diaries to his family, indeed one might even be forgiven for assuming that he had none. Yet, in a letter to his friend Robert Rising of Horsey, Norfolk, he wrote of his fourteen year old son:

simmering in Latin and Greek, while he writes English about as well as a first-rate washerwoman. He positively must not go to Eton until he can write, read and cypher in a finished manner.

The boy swears he'll be nothing but a *music-master*!

Hawker married twice. First at Lisbon in 1811, where he wed Julia, only daughter of Major Hooker Barttelst, by whom he had two sons, and two daughters. His second marriage in 1844 was to Helen Susan, widow of Captain John Symonds, R.N. and daughter of Major Chatterton.

Throughout the diaries of Colonel Peter Hawker, soldier, sportsman, author, musician and country gentleman, entry after entry records illness, suffering and serious operations all brought about by that unlucky bullet at Talavera. Indeed, it seems almost as though he revels in this hypochondria. He goes out shooting when he is as "nervous as a cat", "almost fainting", and "as weak as a chicken". The weather, too, was always in the extreme. The gales were "Siberian", the hail "larger than pigeons' eggs", and the conditions generally "for whales and white bears only".

It is a credit to the man that he spent so much time in pursuit of his beloved sport, although racked with pain, and whilst many may be inclined to scoff at his written records, I would point out that his failures are recorded as accurately as his successes. He writes exactly what he thinks, regardless of whom it may offend.

There is one factor, though, in this amazing man's life which is quite out of keeping with the status of a country gentleman. Colonel Hawker *poached* with the same enthusiasm with which he shot over his own extensive preserves at Longparish! He was a boy at heart, delighting in pranks, and this is the only possible defence which can be offered for behaviour which today would be considered criminal. He was only twenty-eight years of age, when, together with some friends, he carried out an attack on the preserves of his neighbour, Lord Portsmouth. Firstly, Hawker sent servants with pistols to draw off the gamekeeper. Thus, unhindered, the Colonel and his confederates invaded the main coverts. To his own gun that day Hawker recorded twenty-eight pheasants, three partridges and a hare.

The following extracts from his diary seem to substantiate the theory that his poaching exploits were purely of a mischievous nature:

10th February 1806

A jack-snipe, a rabbit and 2 hares. The hares ran out of a hedge together. I killed them right and left in front of Lord Berkeley's house, and while I was hiding under the hedge (fearing a keeper might be on the lookout at hearing the gun) a dragoon ran and picked up both hares, gave a view holla, and held one up in each hand in order to be seen from the window of his Lordship's mansion. Of course, we retreated immediately, and luckily got off unseen.

7th May 1806

In the evening went to Drayton, and killed 40 rooks in about an hour, without missing a shot. The owner of them was at the time gone from home for the purpose of inviting a party to dinner, and to attack the rooking the next day. **In consequence of my slaughter the preceding evening, the whole party killed but three rooks the day after.**

There is no doubt that Colonel Hawker was the finest gameshot who ever lived. He performed the whole of his marksmanship with muzzle loading guns, and one can only speculate on his performance in modern times had he been fortunate enough to live long enough to shoot with modern breech loading weapons. As it was, he shot through fifty-one seasons, chronicling almost every day that he set foot on the fields of Longparish, or pushed off in his punt from Keyhaven.

On September 6th, 1837, he records:

Miraculous shooting again. I was out from ten till five, and came in with 22 partridges and one hare without missing even a long shot or losing a bird. I made five doublets, and by means of three 'cannons' got my 23 head in 20 shots, and many very long shots among them.

In four September days Hawker fired eighty-three shots, missing once, and bagging eighty-nine head of game. He refers to "cannons" in a footnote as "catching two birds as they cross, and then firing so quick as not to allow them to open again".

Colonel Peter Hawker loved to be afloat in his punt in search of wildfowl off Keyhaven at every available opportunity. The more inclement the weather, the better. He despised those who shot their wildfowl from the foreshore, and had a volume of names for them, which he used frequently. They were, vagabonds, butterfly shooters, scoundrels, jealous villains, popping vagrants, jackanapes, reptiles, shore-popping rabble, and rabble of bunglers.

Gradually Hawker's wound began to trouble him more and more, and towards the end of his days he sometimes did not shoot for a whole season. It was during these periods of enforced confinement that he wrote his book of instructions to young sportsmen, cramming it full of all that he had learnt throughout a lifetime of experience. Much of what he advises still applies to this day. Had he not been invalided out of the army at an early age, it would probably never have been written.

Colonel Peter Hawker passed peacefully away on August 7th 1853 at the age of sixty-seven. There are, however, two conflicting accounts of the actual place of his death. One reports that he died at 2, Dorset Place, London, whilst the other favours his country home at Longparish. I prefer to believe the latter, if for no other reason than that it is in sight of his beloved partridge fields. I am sure that is the way Peter Hawker would have wanted it.

CHAPTER 19

Deer

SEASONS FOR DEER

Before you even contemplate a deerstalking expedition, there are two factors which you must fully acquaint yourself with:

1. The open season for *red deer and fallow deer* are as follows:

   Red Deer
   England and Wales:
   1st August–30th April—STAGS
   1st November–28/29th February—HINDS
   Scotland:
   1st July–20th October—STAGS
   21st October–15th February—HINDS

   Fallow Deer
   England and Wales:
   1st August–30th April—BUCKS
   1st November–28th February—DOES
   Scotland:
   1st August–30th April—BUCKS
   21st October–15th February—HINDS

2. Deer can no longer be killed with a shotgun except on private property and where they are doing damage to crops, when they may only be shot with shot sizes Spec. SG or larger. A rifle of no smaller bore than a .240 may be used.

STALKING PROCEDURE

Having established this fact, we can now take a look at some of the points which might make the difference between success and failure when you set foot in a deer forest for the first time. Of course, you may well be accompanied by a professional deerstalker and/or a ghillie. If you are paying handsomely for your sport, then it is a certain factor that you will not be setting out on a lone foray. However, if you happen to be friendly with somebody who happens to have deer on his land, and he gives you permission to go and shoot one, then you want to know something about the procedure beforehand.

It is a fact that almost invariably in fine weather you will find the stags on high ground. When it is wet, they will generally be in the woods lower down. Bearing this in mind, you can often save yourself a few miles of fruitless walking. Deer move up-wind whilst feeding, and during gales they are apt to move anywhere without apparent reason. So, if the wind is almost tearing you off your feet, you stand a fair chance of finding your quarry wherever you go. Of course, as for any type of game, you must never attempt to stalk them down-wind.

Currents of air will move up and down narrow valleys, so if you are on high ground over-looking a herd, note the movement of trees and undergrowth where *they* are. The wind-direction down below may be totally opposite to that where you are lying. When the winds are strong, although deer may move irrationally, the stalk will be much more difficult, for your scent will be conveyed to them plainly. It is a good policy to avoid outlying herds of deer, for if these get your scent, you could find that every deer in the forest is joining them in their retreat.

CARE OF YOUR GLASS
A brief mention of your glass is worthwhile, particularly regarding its care whilst stalking on hill and in forest. It is best kept covered at all times, except when in use, and if the weather is wet, then use it sparingly. A glass which has become fogged up is as bad as having none at all. My own glass is ideal for the purpose, mahogany cased with shutters at either end, a relic of the Napoleonic Wars. However, each time it has been in use, I strip it down, and dry it off thoroughly, for condensation is likely to form on the inside if it is just put away after a damp day.

IMPORTANCE OF A BREEDING STOCK
Most deer forests have a head limit for the season, and if you have a professional stalker with you he will point out which stags you may shoot, and how many. His employer has the welfare of the herd at heart, and often he will instruct that the best stags are left for breeding stock. This latter is not always a policy which is

adhered to, and many deer-forests now have an inferior stock, due to too many fine specimens having been shot in the past.

The worst thing that can happen to any deerstalker is to see his stag bound away wounded after the shot. Inevitably, this will happen to even the best marksman, but every effort must be made to track down and despatch the beast. This, of course, is why there is a strict enforcement of the type of weapon which must be used, for too many deer have died a lingering death from shotgun or small-bore rifle wounds.

DEER POPULATION OF THE BRITISH ISLES

Let us now take a more general look at the deer population throughout the British Isles. Deer are increasing today, and most noteworthy of all is the spread of the Japanese Sika deer. This species, since its original escape from private deer parks, is establishing itself in many parts of the country. Little larger than a hare, it has become a matter of concern to both agriculture and forestry. Twice I have met up with it, in South Shropshire, and Cannock Chase in the Midlands. This latter place is famous for its herds of fallow deer, and sometimes, in the summer months, I enjoy a walk across this large acreage of forest and heather. Twice, I have seen as many as sixty head in an evening, and a few Sika as well.

Obviously, even in a National Trust park such as Cannock Chase, although no deerstalking is permitted, the herds have to be controlled by officials. These men are experts at their job, shooting from specially constructed hides, fully aware, after hours of patient observation beforehand, which stags they wish to eliminate. Shooting at close range, using high-powered rifles with telescopic-sights, they rarely wound.

Advice on Obtaining Stalking

The cost of deerstalking is high. Apart from invitations to large forests, which will not often come the way of the average rough-shooter, some good stalking can be obtained by watching the advertisement columns in the sporting journals. It will not be cheap, perhaps £50 per day, maybe more. However, if you can build yourself a reputation as a reliable and efficient deer-shot, then you may obtain all sorts of very worthwhile invitations. For instance, I know of many gamekeepers, on whose land there are sizeable herds of deer. It will be their responsibility to control these, and once you have proved yourself in this respect, you will often be called upon, year after year.

DEER POACHING

There is, though, a far from sporting aspect of deer-shooting, and one which we may read of in the national press, usually in a small insignificant paragraph. I refer, of course, to *poaching,* an evil which is increasing each year, despite attempts by the authorities to curb it. It is, undoubtedly, the most vile of all rural crimes.

Deer poaching is mostly carried out from vehicles at night, usually Land Rovers which can leave the road if necessity demands. Seldom is it just a "lark" entered into with a misguided spirit of adventure. Instead, it is a highly organised business, operated by ruthless men, often prepared to commit murder if surprised by a lone warden. They have a market to supply, with carcases averaging £60-70 each. Consequently, a night's "work" can be extremely rewarding from a financial point of view. They may operate several nights each week, subsequent raids being a hundred or more miles apart. Areas such as Cannock Chase, with miles of remote, unfenced roads are ideal for their purpose. All too often, they use shotguns, rifles being difficult to sight in the headlights of a vehicle, particularly if they have to shoot whilst moving. They have one idea in mind, namely to locate a herd of deer as close to the road as possible, and to blast into them with twelve bores. More will be wounded than killed! Often these poachers will take advantage of moonlight nights, when they can traverse moorland adjoining woods, without using their headlights. Once they have fired a barrage of shots, usually at such close range that it is virtually impossible to miss, they will haul the slain aboard as quickly as possible, and then head for home. They will not dream of pursuing the wounded deer, and it is hoped that these poor beasts will either die quickly, or else be found by a warden next morning, when they will be quickly despatched.

In these turbulent times, the police force have far too much crime to cope with in the towns than to spend time on speculative patrols for deer poachers. Therefore, it is left to the wardens and gamekeepers to combat this menace as best they can. It is, indeed, a brave man (nay, foolish!) who will tackle one of these gangs single-handed. His best method is to approach unseen and, having located the poachers, telephone for help from the nearest available source. It is almost a certainty that the registration plates on the vehicle will be false. However, in remote areas if a police road-block can be set up quickly, the criminals have little chance of escaping. Even should they manage to dispose of their loot and weapons before being apprehended, there will be evidence of their mission inside the vehicle. A few stains of deer's blood, or a spent cartridge case, will be sufficient to convict them. The penalties are severe. Even ordinary night poaching, between the hours of sunset and sunrise, carries a maximum penalty of six months' imprisonment, so the deer poacher will not escape lightly, particularly when unlicensed firearms are used. This, however, serves to make them all the more desperate!

DEER ON FORESTRY COMMISSION LAND

All Forestry Commission leases for sporting-rights exclude the right to kill deer. Likewise, they forbid the use of rifles on their land. This, again, is another bid to increase deer conservation, and to eliminate suffering. I well remember, one snowy day, whilst shooting on my acreage in the Shropshire/Welsh border hills with a colleague, discovering a set of cloven prints leading out from amidst the conifer thickets. A sudden thrill coursed through my veins. Had the rapidly spreading Sika deer found my land at last? Although we had no intention of shooting the animal, we decided to try to track it down out of curiosity. On and on went those footprints in the snow, maintaining an almost direct course along the snow covered Forestry Commission roads. Finally, two miles farther on, it terminated at a gap in a very rusty wire-netting fence alongside a sheep-field. There, just inside the field, bleating plaintively, was the trespasser on my shoot, a large ewe, very much in lamb!

HIGH ACCIDENT RATE OF DEER KILLED ON ROADS

Something which I have not mentioned so far is the very high accident rate of deer on our roads. How often have we seen that road-sign which warns us of the danger of these animals ahead. I wonder how many people reduce their speed accordingly. Not many, I would think. No more than those who blatantly disregard the possibility of straying cattle. Yet, these people, whom we must regard as being completely selfish and ignorant, are totally unaware of the damage which they can do to themselves, and their vehicle, if they happen to collide with a deer. Almost nightly, somewhere in these islands of ours, a deer limps into the thickets, maimed and bleeding after an encounter with a car. And the driver? He curses the poor animal fluently, whilst inspecting the damage to his vehicle, without a thought to the suffering he has caused by his careless driving. Unfortunately, there is little we can do to prevent this constant danger to our herds of deer, except by additional fencing, the amount and cost of which would be impracticable. Even if this were possible, it would be yet another means of destroying the freedom of a wild animal which is part of our heritage.

I am convinced that the deer will spread to my own shoot within the next two or three years. When they arrive, I shall welcome them, and afford them all the protection within my power. I sincerely hope that this is the ideal of every rough-shooter worthy of having land under his control. They must not be regarded as a quarry to be pursued at every available opportunity, but rather as an investment.

CHAPTER 20

Grouse and Blackgame

I shot for fifteen years before I finally bagged my first grouse and blackcock, killing both on the same day. The beginner will probably groan with dismay on hearing this, but, by way of encouragement, I would add that I had only been on a grouse-moor twice before in my life. The average rough-shooter will seldom come across them, except when shooting on high ground, with these birds specifically the quarry. Seldom does one encounter them on lowlands during the course of an ordinary day's sport.

GROUSE

The grouse is yet another bird surrounded by an aura of mystery. Its movements, from moor to moor, are unpredictable. It is a game-bird which is very much at the mercy of Nature, and, unlike the pheasant and the partridge, is not hand-reared extensively. However, game-farms are experimenting, reasonably successfully, in rearing grouse in captivity, although the expense involved will be way beyond the pocket of the average game-preserver, as will this type of shooting, generally.

Importance of Heather Burning

The quality of the heather in various parts of the country largely affects the movement of grouse, for this is their staple diet. A moorland gamekeeper is responsible for "muir-burning", i.e., burning off of certain acres of heather, so that a new growth of young tender shoots may be encouraged. However, this process is governed by law, and, in most areas, it is forbidden after 31st March, presumably so that nesting birds will not be burned. Muir burning is not quite so simple as it sounds, requiring much more planning than setting forth with a box of matches during a spell of dry weather! Indeed, if the keeper concerned is not careful, he might set the whole moor alight, to the detriment of grouse, blackgame and sheep.

In Times of Hard Weather

It is during times of hard weather that the grouse population suffers. With the heather buried below several feet of packed snow, the birds will starve unless they receive help of some kind. Unfortunately, they cannot be fed like pheasants and partridge. The keeper must attempt to clear an area of snow, and expose some heather for them. He can, however, distribute grit on his moor, for this is another essential of the grouse.

The Scarcity of Grouse Shooting

The beginner may well wonder how he can obtain some grouse shooting. Of course, one often sees advertisements inviting tenders for an acreage of unkeepered grouse-moor. Rents may vary from £1 to £5 per acre, but you are rarely likely to find a bargain these days. Landowners, with a few acres of heather and sheep-grazing, will advertise it as a grouse moor, and furthermore, they will get their price! I well remember one morning as I was coming off the merse after a fruitless flight, being stopped by a fellow wildfowler, hitherto a perfect stranger to myself. After discussing a few general topics, he asked me outright if I would be interested in accompanying himself, and two companions, on a day's grouse shooting. His shoot was some seventy miles to the north, whilst he came from two hundred miles to the south! He had taken this land on a 3-year lease, content to pay his rent, but only take advantage of the sporting potentials of couple of times during the season. Furthermore, he had not yet set foot on his new shoot, the transaction having been conducted through the post! I was fully aware, of course, why I had been singled out for an invitation. I had a dog, and none of the other three owned one between them!

The one consolation of that day was the gorgeous October sunshine. It was very pleasant, indeed, to walk the heather-covered hills, allowing Remus to range to and fro in front of me. I fired the only shot of the day, killing a high woodpigeon, the one species of wildlife which we saw all day! I never even saw any grouse droppings, something which I was constantly on the lookout for. Somehow, I don't think my host of that day will be renewing his lease when it expires!

Yet, I had my first introduction to grouse-shooting on such a place as this, and enjoyed a day's sport which I shall never forget. During my many stays on the Solway Firth, I have nearly always resided at the Nith Hotel, in Glencaple, owned by Billy Houliston of soccer fame. Apart from the excellent cuisine, this hotel has much to offer in the way of rough-shooting.

A Visit to Manquhill

It was in this way that I came to shoot at Manquhill, a "lost valley" necessitating a three mile drive over rutted cart-tracks between towering hills, before arriving at one's destination. It was, truly, the most splendid surroundings in which I have ever shot. There were only three of us on that particular day and, once again, I was merely anticipating a pleasant day spent in congenial surroundings. However, once we had ascended the steep valley, and had reached the wide plateau above, I began to realise that there was a distinct possibility that I might shoot my first grouse.

The terrain was boggy, and the going was heavy. We could hear grouse and, from time to time, two or three would hurtle out of a patch of heather. They were very wild though, no doubt due to the fact that parties of guests from the hotel were pursuing them weekly.

I was more than delighted when, eventually, I knocked one down out of a small covey with my second barrel. The afternoon advanced, and, as we made our way back in the direction of the parked vehicle, it seemed that our total bag would stand at the single grouse which I had shot, and three rabbits accounted for by my companions.

However, less than half a mile from the car stood a small, isolated hillock, amongst the heather, the grass upon it seeming emerald green in contrast to the brown background. My colleagues suggested that I should walk over it, whilst they worked the dogs along the base. Consequently, any rabbits which they put up would bolt uphill towards me.

As I neared the summit of this small hill, I was taken by surprise as something suddenly exploded to life on the apparently bare ground in front of me. I caught a glimpse of a dark shape hurtling upwards, and then collapsing in mid-air, as my instinctive snap-shot halted its flight. I had claimed my first blackcock!

BLACKGAME

Blackgame are virtually a larger version of the grouse, their habits being very similar, although they are usually found singly, or in pairs, rather than in coveys. I recently drove through a hill farm in Scotland where a couple of these birds were sunning themselves on the lawn in front of the house! Apparently they are the favourite pets of the farmer's wife, and they take advantage of the security offered around the farm.

The following season I paid a return visit to Manquhill, this time on my own, for my hotel friends were unable to accompany me. Again, I was favoured with sunshine, as I set out on a lone foray on this 3,000 acres. Never have I felt so over-awed, alone in this remote place, one man and a dog pitting their wits against the might of nature. All I saw that day was one covey of grouse, springing up on the slopes below me, and gliding, effortlessly over the stone walls below. Yet I was glad that I had returned to renew my acquaintance with a place which will live in my memory forever, along with that blackcock's tail-feather, carefully pressed between the pages of my favourite shooting book.

Grouse, however, are not confined to Scotland alone, although the denser populations are to be found there. Several good grouse-moors are also to be found in Wales, and even on the outskirts of the midlands on Cannock Chase.

CAPERCAILLIE

Another bird worthy of mention in this chapter is the capercaillie, found almost exclusively in Scotland at heights above 1,000 feet. The caper, however, does not feed on heather, but relies on the shoots of fir trees for its staple diet. It was this factor which turned my thoughts towards the possibility of an experiment, some years ago. If capercaillie exist 1,000 ft. above sea-level, and require conifer forests, why could they not survive on my hill-shoot on the Shropshire/Welsh borders, where similar conditions exist? Consequently, I wrote letters to the Forestry Commission, and to several Scottish game-farms engaged on experiments with grouse. The Commission welcomed my idea, and could see no reason why the birds should not take to these woods. However, my stumbling block came from one of the game-farms (the only reply I received to six separate queries) who regretted being unable to help me at the present, as they were conducting their own experiments regarding capers in captivity. Stock birds were scarce, and they were unable to supply me with any until their scheme had progressed. I am still waiting. Perhaps, one day, I shall introduce the first pair of capercaillie to these border hills.

PTARMIGAN

We must not overlook the ptarmigan, that "snow bird" of the Scottish highlands. Very few rough-shooters come into contact with this very fine sporting bird, unless they deliberately set out to do so. This type of shooting requires a degree of physical fitness far beyond that necessitated by the average shooting man. The terrain will consist of steep, rock strewn slopes, where every foothold is precarious. The ptarmigan has the gift of blending itself into a snowy background, and springing at that very moment when the shooter least expects it. If one is fully fit, then, apart from wildfowling, there is no finer sport.

Thus, we have deviated from the rough-shooter's average programme. We have taken a peep into the wilder, more inaccessible parts of these islands, at birds which, to date, have no artificiality in their existence. Yet, we are still responsible for their well-being, for, as conservationists, the welfare of all wildlife is in our own interests. We must account for it to the next generation.

CHAPTER 21

Poachers

DISAPPEARANCE OF THE "MOOCHER"

One character who has almost disappeared from the rural scene is the village poacher. He belongs to an age which has now passed, and no longer do we see this fellow lurking in the country lanes throughout the daylight hours, plotting and planning his nocturnal forays, or idling in the public houses at mid-day, his ears trained to pick up any gossip from the farm labourers concerning the whereabouts of fur or feather on the estates.

These poachers were well-known amongst the local community. Whilst despised by the gamekeepers and police, on account of the extra hours of watchfulness which their very way of life necessitated in the coverts, landowners were apt to treat them with a fair amount of tolerance when compared with their modern mobile counterparts of this present day. They helped themselves to what game they required to feed their own families, hoping also for a "bonus" for which they had a ready market, but the disturbance which they caused in heavily stocked pheasant preserves was negligible. Far better to lose a few birds, which would not really be missed anyway, than to have the entire lot scattered over the parish due to the clumsy efforts of some hit and run raider with a shotgun.

A Dying Breed of Poacher

I was talking to one of these old-time poachers, only a few weeks ago. He is small of stature, with a peaked cap pulled down over his gaunt face, and a navy blue overcoat, reaching almost to his ankles. I can never remember seeing him without this latter garment, summer or winter. It serves as a hiding place for many things from a freshly killed rabbit to a home-made catapult . . . but never a gun!

Old Joe is well into his seventies now and, in his own words, he has "turned respectable". He has permission to ferret rabbits out

The modern poacher. Shooting from the road with .22 rifle and telescopic sight

of the hedgerows bordering the playing-fields of a nearby school, but the fact that he invariably strays on to the surrounding farmland is of little consequence to him. In the old days, he would have been termed a "moocher", a regular nuisance to the local keepers, but no real threat to the game population.

I remember once taking him down to my own shoot in order that he might assist me in trying to check a rapidly increasing rabbit population. Dawn had not yet broken on a snowy December morning, when I pulled up in the street of terraced houses in which he lived. I had not had time to switch off the engine before he appeared in the porch of his house, where he informed me he had been waiting for the past half-hour, although I had arrived on time! His hands were thrust deep into the pockets of this capacious coat, and in reply to my query, he assured me that both ferrets, and his "snap" were in there also!

It was not a successful venture as far as ferreting was concerned, for by mid-day we had reached the conclusion that the coneys were not in their warrens, but were lying out in the undergrowth. A couple of hours of beating through this thick terrain proved our theory to be correct, and also produced a fairly respectable bag of rabbits to take home with us. However, my old friend was far from happy. He did not care for this wild place in the Shropshire hills, preferring the friendly surroundings of his native cricket and football fields, in close proximity to the ale-houses. His final comment, at the end of the day, summed it all up, "I wouldn't c'mere to die", he stated, with heartfelt sincerity.

Whilst not condoning the way of life of my old friend, I confess that I miss these characters who were born and bred in the outlying villages. Old Joe related to me many of his early exploits, the usual tales of lying prone in deep undergrowth, whilst the gamekeepers searched for him. These yarns usually have a smattering of truth in them, but over the years their telling becomes as colourful as the one who relates them.

Secrets of an Old Poacher
However, Joe did part with a few of his "trade secrets", and I have no reason to doubt the authenticity of the methods he used. It only served to make me realise how unnecessary is a gun for the sole purpose of taking game, and the object of the exercise being to provide rabbits and pheasants, either for the table or for sale, the sporting aspect not entering into it.

I heard the tale of how he took a whole covey of partridges one day, within a few hundred yards of the keeper's cottage. Having patrolled the lanes during the daylight hours, the old poacher had noticed the birds flying into this rough grass field at night to "juk". Consequently, he soaked a cupful of wheat in whiskey, and scattered this in close proximity to the place, after darkness. Long before dawn he was crouched behind the straggling hawthorn hedge, watching and waiting.

He had not long to wait, however, for within twenty minutes of daybreak, fifteen partridges were fluttering and rolling about, completely helpless under the influence of the whiskey. His stout ash stick ensured that he had a full "hare pocket" on his return home, and he sat down to a hearty breakfast, made all the more enjoyable by the thought that there would be a few extra shillings to spare in his household that week.

Similarly, he robbed that same estate of a few pheasants just prior to Christmas, only this time his methods were much more cruel. He spent a few hours, one evening, drilling holes through a quantity of dried peas. He then threaded each one with a length of stout horsehair, leaving a quarter of an inch protruding at either end. These were duly scattered outside a wood which adjoined a public footpath, and once again old Joe left his bed early, in order to inspect the fruits of his labours. He picked up six fully grown pheasants that morning, all of which his faithful old lurcher, Midnight, found choking to death in the surrounding bracken. Harsh methods, but effective, nevertheless.

POACHERS' DOGS

Most of the old-time poachers were at once identified by their inseparable companions, their dogs. Mostly these followed a pattern of a cross between a collie and a greyhound or whippet. The cunning of the former, combined with the speed of the latter, was invaluable in the taking of game during the hours of darkness. Nets were often used to secure large bags of rabbits when poaching on open grass fields, and an intelligent dog could be trained to make a detour, and drive the rabbits into the net, where its master was waiting to pounce on them. However, this method was not always practicable, for the keepers would combat this by planting thorn bushes at intervals, thwarting the drag-netter, and limiting the places where the system could be used, thereby making night-patrolling much easier.

My old friend is one of the survivors of a dying race. Nowadays he is well satisfied with a couple of rabbits for half a day's work. He is well cared for in his old age, and has neither the inclination, nor the need to poach seriously. The modern poacher, operating from a car, tours the country lanes at weekends, taking pot-shots at any form of wildlife, whether game or protected birds. He has no regard for close seasons, no respect for man nor beast, and this, coupled with a complete ignorance of the rural way of life, is one of the biggest threats to our countryside today. Give me the old poacher any day. Whatever his drawbacks, his was a natural way of life, a part of the true rural picture.

NEW LEGISLATION

The *Armed Trespass Act 1968* has now made poaching a criminal offence, and the police can enter land to apprehend an offender without permission from the landowner. No longer does "trespassing in pursuit of game" have to be proved. The very fact that a man is trespassing with a firearm is sufficient to bring about a prosecution.

However, let us take a look at one or two instances of civil trespass, whether intentional on the part of the offender or not.

Many years ago, before I was fortunate enough to rent the shooting of several hundred acres of land in the beautiful Shropshire/Welsh border hills, my sporting rights were situated in close proximity to the industrial Midlands. Poaching and trespassing were evils which I encountered only too frequently, and I came to accept them as something which had to be dealt with when the occasion arose, but could never be eliminated. Prosecutions were the order of the day and weekends were devoted mostly to patrolling one's ground on the lookout for these nuisances. Shooting was generally arranged to take place on weekdays when, with luck, one could pursue one's chosen sport uninterrupted.

However, within months of the tenancy of my hill shoot above Clun, the absence of this continual "invasion" from the urban areas was only too apparent. It was a wonderful feeling, indeed, to be able to spend a full day on the place without once having to take somebody to task over some law of the countryside which they had, possibly unwittingly, broken. In due course I lapsed into a state of false security, and when I caught my first poacher there, I was rather inclined to look upon him as the one black sheep of the area.

TRESPASS

Trespassing is a controversial subject in any part of the British Isles. The offender always firmly believes that he cannot be prosecuted so long as he has done no damage. He is right up to a point, but the law states that a trespasser may be requested to leave the land, and if he fails to do so, then he may be removed, using no more force than is necessary. The tenant or land-owner must determine the amount of force to be used, and anything in excess of this could lead to a court case with himself facing a charge of assault. Now, a person who has been ordered to leave land where he has no right to be, has no option other than to depart. Failure to do so, or a return visit, will involve him in trouble with the police. He has made a nuisance of himself just as much as a hooligan at a football match who resists attempts to put him out of the ground. This is very fair, for it protects the person who has genuinely trespassed in error, and the position can be clarified without further repercussions.

Trespassing in the hills is a minor nuisance compared to that which exists in more densely populated areas. I find that the weather plays a predominant part in the amount of "trouble" I can expect at weekends. During a spell of fine weather, which we experience from time to time during the summer months, I can usually guarantee that the piece of waste ground on the roadside, adjoining my main woodlands, will be devoid of cars at weekends. The reason for this is that the city dwellers, realising that the weather is settled for a few days at least, have made up their minds to travel the extra sixty miles to the coast. They have probably reached this decision during the latter part of the previous week, on hearing the weather forecast for the next few days. On the other hand, if the weather shows signs of clearing up after a week of wind and rain, I can guarantee that my "car park" will be full. In this case, no plans have been made for a weekend trip to the sea, but with the advent of fine weather suddenly at the end of the week, the motorist decides on a shorter trip into the country. Naturally, on a weekend of incessant rain, I can expect to see nobody at all, but this does not make it any the more pleasant for me.

Most of the time, the motorists who have pulled on to this piece of waste ground are content to remain there, for they have a very pleasant view of the Radnorshire hills in front of them, whereas, if they enter the woodlands, the surrounding scenery is screened from their view by the thickets of artificially planted trees. However, the occasional thoughtless visitor to these parts sees my land as the ideal place to exercise his unruly dog, without the hazards of passing traffic. He is most indignant when I point out to him the error of his ways, and generally replies that he has not brought a leash with him, so he is unable to comply with my request to keep the dog under control. I have the answer to this frequent situation when I produce a length of twine from my game bag, and demand that he uses this until he is clear of my boundaries!

One can usually find a ready-made excuse to evict a troublesome trespasser, and I quote one classic example which occurred in the early part of last year. I spotted a man and his family one afternoon, along one of the main forestry rides, with a Jack Russell Terrier ranging to and fro at will. I approached them in order to remonstrate with them, when I noticed something which gave me far greater grounds for complaint than the roving dog. The man had a spade under his arm, and was carrying a young broom tree which he had obviously just dug up to replant in his garden. During the ensuing conversation I reminded him that, worthless as this shrub might appear to be to him, it was an offence to remove *anything* from somebody else's land without prior permission. The question of the unruly dog never arose, for I knew full well that I should never see him on my land again.

Poaching, on the whole, is isolated in the Clun area. I have had three court cases in thirteen years, which speaks for itself. I never believe in letting poachers off with a warning. This may seem a hard line to take, but I have learned by my mistakes in the past. A hardened poacher regards a warning as a weakness on the part of the man who catches him, and it merely serves to make him more stealthy in the future. If you let him go, you never know how long it will be before you manage to catch him again, and by then he may have helped himself to an awful lot of your game.

This border county is one of the best areas I have ever rented shooting rights in with regard to freedom from poachers and trespassers. It is this which makes the isolated instances, when they occur, seem far worse than they really are. Fortunately, I do not keep to a regular pattern regarding days and times for visiting my own land, and the sneak poacher, who tries to take advantage of my absence, will never be able to do so without the occasional glance over his shoulder. It is the duty of every true countryman to report to the owner of any land upon which he sees either poaching or trespassing taking place. Only in this way can we all appreciate the countryside around us, by preserving the wildlife and beauty from the depredations of those to whom the word conservation is meaningless.

CHAPTER 22

Experiments
in Conservation

THE MARCH OF "PROGRESS"

It was with great sadness in my heart that I clambered slowly up the old pit-mound, slipping back one yard for every two that I gained, until, eventually, with my breath coming in short gasps, I gained the summit. The sun was warm, encouraging clouds of midges to hang over the blackish, seemingly bottomless, pools which lay behind me. In front of me, there was some three hundred acres or so of flooded water-meadows, adjoining these open-cast coal workings, with moorhens and grebes covering the surface, their constant jerking movements making them seem as though they were artificial replicas propelled by clockwork. Far out in the centre, somewhere, the River Anker followed its sluggish course, discernible only by slight rippling movements on the otherwise stagnant surface.

My heart was heavy because I had known this place so long ago, in the days before drilling and mining were even contemplated. I can visualise that familiar scene even whilst gazing out across this ugly, scarred landscape. The river was just a narrow, muddy channel in those days, choked in places by thick reed-beds, and the mallard bred here, undisturbed. Once a Bittern was heard to boom throughout the still, summer evenings, whilst it sat its eggs, hatched its young, and then disappeared, never to return again. The swans used to favour that part of the Anker which passed close to the "Pretty Pigs" Inn, for the fishermen and their families, who visited it at weekends, would bring the stale bread and crusts which they had accumulated during the previous week, and feed these majestic birds.

Yes, this was the Alvecote I once knew, a place where time seemed to stand still, and man was almost an intruder in a land which belonged to Nature herself. Once it was owned by Harry Brown, the famous racehorse owner, and close friend of Edward VII, then Prince of Wales. He shot the whole of the surrounding

A ringed swan   Photo: Guy Smith

farmlands, and I can remember the elaborate duck "hides" which he built along the river banks, with raised wooden floors so that his royal guest might keep his feet dry, whilst waiting for a shot at flighting mallard and teal.

Then, for some reason, Harry Brown sold these Alvecote meadows, the whole three hundred acres realising no more than £400! The tenant farmers now purchased the fields they had once rented, but apart from that, there was no visible change. I managed to take the shooting rights of a couple of these water meadows, situated between the narrow country road and the river. By this time, the wooden hides were rotting, and unsafe, so I used to crouch behind the trunk of a fallen willow tree, patiently listening for the magical wingbeats of mallard, and the shrill, piping whistle of teal.

Thus it continued for some years. My memories are happy ones, of my dogs, Dutch, Jetta and Mac, and of the balmy August evening, so very long ago, when I shot my first mallard, killing it stone dead on the wing with the luckiest shot I have ever fired. A single pellet of SSG struck it below the beak as it rocketed over me, and Jetta, then almost blind, plunged into the jungle of bullrushes, and retrieved it for me.

However, nothing remains unchanged for long in this day and age, and one morning I noticed that some strange, and very large, items of machinery had appeared on the opposite side of the river to where I shot. Drilling for coal had commenced. It continued for some weeks, and then the men gathered up their equipment and departed. They were not seen again for a couple of years and, I must confess, I had been lulled into a false sense of optimistic security. Perhaps they had failed to discover seams of coal beneath the surface of this quiet rural backwater. Yet, the wheels of industry grind slowly, missing nothing.

Those Alvecote meadows were mined relentlessly and ruthlessly. The old farm house, up on the hill, was demolished without any sentiment, and the surrounding pools were drained in the process. The countryside was fighting a losing battle against an invincible foe, yet Nature struck back in her own inimitable way.

The flooding began some months later, and the industrial bastion fell. The whole structure beneath the surface refused to tolerate the disturbances of man any longer, and it was the River Anker, which burst its banks in defiance. Within weeks, every hollow and crevice was filled with black, lifeless water, and the scene was changed yet again. I continued shooting as before, although my own area of dry land was reduced almost to pocket-handkerchief size, and the water on which the wildfowl now settled was so vast that fewer and fewer came within range of my gun.

THE MAKING OF A NATURE RESERVE

Then I was struck another blow, although it was actually in the interests of the wildlife of the area. The Wildfowl Trust were taking over Alvecote, and turning it into a Nature Reserve. I would be able to shoot there no longer. This process was far more gradual than had been the open-cast coalmining. The outsider was unaware that anything at all was happening, apart from the notice-boards which urged one not to pick flowers, damage trees, etc.

Within five years, one of the finest inland Nature Reserves in the country had been created. Apart from bird-life, insects proved to be the most startling feature of the fields and woods surrounding the floodwater. Rare spiders were discovered in an old orchard, and species of butterflies, hitherto unseen in the midlands, flitted to and fro.

However, the wildfowl population was soon trebled. With the advent of winter, rafts of wigeon appeared, like fleets of jet-planes, streaking down to settle in the middle of this flooded area, in the knowledge that they were safe here. Canada geese were seen more frequently, and once a Pinkfoot rested there for three days, during migration.

So Alvecote settled down in its new role over the following years. Some of us accepted it as a permanency, and realised that we had gained something of far greater value in exchange for the loss of our own particular sporting pursuits.

However, a reverse situation has occurred on another expanse of water, not so very far away from this important sanctuary.

THE DESTRUCTION OF A NATURAL RESERVE

In the heart of the industrial midlands, fifteen miles north of Birmingham, stands the small township of Chasetown. Here is the home of Chasewater, a lake seven miles in circumference, a popular resort at weekends for the people from the surrounding urban areas. Up until a few years ago very few outside the immediate locality knew of its existence, and to those who were aware of it, it was just one more piece of floodwater caused by mining subsidence.

Then, a few years ago, a sailing club was formed there, and within a few weeks the "quiet times" of Chasewater were over. Water-ski-ing followed, and national sailing events were organised during the summer months. Part of the surrounding marshy ground found itself under concrete, a residents' recreation area was built with swings and various other amusements for the young, and in a very short space of time this peaceful inland water had taken on a new look.

However, all was not well with Chasewater. It was very convenient for the visitor who envisaged a day out in pleasant surroundings, with possibly a regatta to watch, but the most important feature of the place had been destroyed. Prior to these inevitable disturbances, "the pool" as it is known locally, had been an unofficial sanctuary for many different species of wildfowl. Only a very severe spell of weather would completely freeze the water, and in a moderate winter it was possible to see flocks of mallard, wigeon and teal sheltering out in the centre, seeking refuge from the gales and blizzards which had driven them there. Migrant wild geese showed up, from time to time, also, pausing

A pair of Canada Geese. Stock birds for breeding

Photo: Guy Smith

there for a well earned rest, on their long journey north or south, according to the time of year. Canada geese enjoyed a stay there for longer periods, and indeed, it was a most interesting place for both the ornithologist and wildfowler.

There had always been shooting on Chasewater, in just the same way as the local gunner may visit it occasionally today. The local council remained indifferent as far as this was concerned, neither encouraging nor preventing the sportsman, for it made very little difference in the long run. Few birds were shot, for they had gained sufficient height to be out of effective shotgun range by the time they reached the land, but there was always a chance of one bird being a little lower than the rest, and occasionally a fluke shot would come off, serving to encourage the rest of the gunners.

AN OLD CHASEWATER 'FOWLER

I was talking to one of the old Chasewater 'fowlers some time ago, and he related to me many tales of the shooting there, in the days between the two wars, when the winter wildfowl population was at its peak. He has long since put away his gun, but one particular story which he told me will always remain in my mind, a memory

207

of the days when there was a lighter side to sport, and more time to enjoy it.

Old Walter was a young man in those days, well-built with a rugged face, who chewed twist incessantly. He was a miner at one of the nearby collieries, his only real interest in life was roaming the "common land" around Chasetown, in search of rabbits, principally, but always keen to have a shot at anything else which presented itself. Joe, his constant companion, both at work and during leisure hours, had the same outlook on life, only that he was less fortunate in possessing only a single-barrelled gun, a formidable weapon, both to himself and his quarry, its split stock bound up with wire, and its rusty barrel wafer thin with both age and use.

The snow lay deep on the ground, and the stars in the sky above sparkled brightly, as these two men met in one of the local ale-houses for their nightly quart of beer.

"I heered geese on pool, tonight as I came across," Joe stated phlegmatically, attempting to light his stubby pipe for the umpteenth time, without success.

"Did'st ye!" Walter replied, his pale blue eyes speaking volumes. "Best drink up then, lad."

The two of them drained their glasses, each knowing what was in the other's mind, and then, placing their empties on the bar in front of them, they turned, and made their way out into the frosty night air.

Half an hour later found the two men forcing their way through the deep snow in the direction of Chasewater. There was just enough light to see to shoot by, at distances up to thirty yards, anyway. Suddenly, they stopped. There was no mistaking the deep "honk" of a goose somewhere ahead of them in the darkness. It was obvious to both men that the birds would be on the one unfrozen stretch of water on the Brownhills side, where today, the funfair stands. They also knew that there was only one chance of getting a shot. One of them would have to remain on the canal side, whilst the other made a detour, coming up behind the birds, and then putting them up. A hurried discussion followed, and it was agreed that old Walter would stay where he was, as he had the "double", and stood more chance, whilst Joe went and flushed the birds.

It was a long cold wait, even for a man of Walter's constitution, and his very blood seemed to freeze as he stamped his feet, and blew on his coarse, gnarled hands. Time seemed to stand still, but in actual fact it was only twenty minutes or so, before he heard the resounding "boom" of Joe's dilapidated old weapon as, having reached the required position, he fired a shot into the night air to put the geese on the move.

The silence was shattered instantly. The air was full of rushing wingbeats. Mallard quacked, wigeon and teal whistled, and, somewhere, geese gaggled . . .

Suddenly, Walter heard heavy wingbeats approaching, and, dimly silhouetted against the starry sky above, he saw four large birds, long necks stretched out in front of them. This was it, the moment he had been waiting for. His gun was at his shoulder, and the two deep "booms" sounded almost as one. Temporarily, he lost sight of his quarry as they passed on into the stygian blackness. He almost feared that he had missed, and then his ears caught the rewarding thump of a heavy bird crashing on to the frozen snow, a hundred yards or so behind him.

Walter was still searching for his goose when Joe joined him.

"Got one," Walter shouted. "Can't find the beggar, though."

They hunted for another ten minutes, and then there was a shout of triumph, a muffled curse, and a burst of laughter from Joe.

"Here it be," he roared, almost unable to contain his mirth. "It ain't no goose, though, ye old fool. You bin' and shot a b—— old swan!"

"I ain't?"

"You 'ev!"

Those were the old days on Chasewater, the days of the real old characters, the wildfowl, and the unspoilt countryside. All this has gone now, replaced by high-speed boats, yachts, hydro-planes and noisy roundabouts, all of which attract crowds of people to the area, whilst driving away the bird life. Unfortunately, the choice is not ours. We must accept that which we are given. This is the reason why the old Chasewater has gone forever, leaving only memories for those who really care.

THE IMPORTANCE OF CONSERVATION

Likewise, we must take an interest in not only our sporting birds and beasts, but wildlife in general. Perhaps such places as Alvecote compensate us for the loss of the old Chasewater. Only the birds themselves know that. We must look upon our shooting as a means of *increasing and protecting* our countryside, and not destroying it. We must pass on our knowledge, and help to educate others. Then, and only then, shall we know the satisfaction of a job well done. It will have been worth the effort.

Appendix

THE WILDLIFE AND COUNTRYSIDE ACT 1981

Various changes were brought about in the *Wildlife and Countryside Act 1981* which the sportsman and amateur gamekeeper must make himself familiar with. Ignorance of the law is no excuse for a breach of the law, and unless the following points are adhered to the reader could find himself facing prosecution.

Protected species
Several species have now been added to the protected list. In spite of its prolific numbers, the curlew is one of these which surprisingly suffered this fate, along with the bar-tailed godwit, redshank and jacksnipe. *The only wader which is now legitimate quarry is the golden plover.*

Other species which were formerly on the wildfowler's quarry list are now also protected, namely the garganey and the bean goose. Cormorant and goosander which were shot in the interests of fisheries can now only be shot under a special licence.

Whitefronted geese are protected in *Scotland*. This ban on shooting was introduced to conserve the Greenland species, but they can be shot elsewhere.

Barnacle geese are, of course, still protected, but where they are doing extensive damage to crops a licence to shoot them can be obtained, but first attempts have to be made to scare them off the area. The licence only permits shooting by four people.

The gamekeeper
There are now some restrictions which will affect the gamekeeper, both amateur and professional.
1. Self-locking snares are now illegal. All free-running snares must be inspected at least once daily.
2. It is illegal to kill hedgehogs, wildcats, polecats and pine martens in either snares or traps.

3. Deer can no longer be shot with a shotgun except on private property and where they are doing damage to crops. Likewise it is still illegal to kill deer with a .22 rifle.

Automatic and semi-automatic weapons
Automatic weapons have been illegal in Great Britain since 1968. There is a restriction on semi-automatic shotguns in so much that the magazine must be blanked off so that one cartridge is in the breech and only two in the magazine. This, however, can be unplugged for vermin shooting but it is illegal to shoot polecats, wildcats, or pine martens with an unplugged gun.

Semi-automatic shotguns can be used for game-shooting provided that they are plugged as mentioned above.

Sale of dead birds
Only feral pigeons and woodpigeons may be sold at any time. Mallard, teal, wigeon, pintail, tufted duck, coot, snipe, woodcock, capercaillie and golden plover may only be sold from September 1st to February 28th. Pheasant, partridge and grouse are still covered by the Game Acts. *The reader is reminded that the sale of dead wild geese is illegal at any time.*

Responsibility
The *Wildlife and Countryside Act* covers many aspects of country life, and it is particularly important that anyone involved in gamekeeping or shooting should be conversant with the requirements of the *Act*. The list of protected species may well be amended from time to time, so it is essential to check the latest position. **It is always the responsibility of the individual to know what the law requires, so if in doubt, check it.**